rover

Greatest Sits Edition

By Andrew Grant & Amanda Hedlund

Every year millions of cats and dogs enter pet rescues in the United States. Only a small percentage are adopted and the fate of the rest is heartbreaking.

Those stats inspired Andrew Grant to produce *Rover* to raise money for and bring awareness to rescues. Andrew photographed over 600 dogs while producing four editions of *Rover* in five years. His efforts generated donations of over one million dollars to rescues across the country. This is a collection of Andrew's favorite images.

Most of the dogs featured in this book once lived in a shelter or rescue. Some were living in a rescue when they were photographed.

Rover beautifully illustrates that there are healthy, smart, fun, loving mixed breeds and purebreds available for adoption in rescues. Andrew hopes the loving faces gracing these pages will inspire you to welcome a shelter pet into your home.

"Pets provide us with unconditional love and priceless moments of joy. They only ask for a home in return. This book is dedicated to all those who help pets find their way home." – Andrew Grant

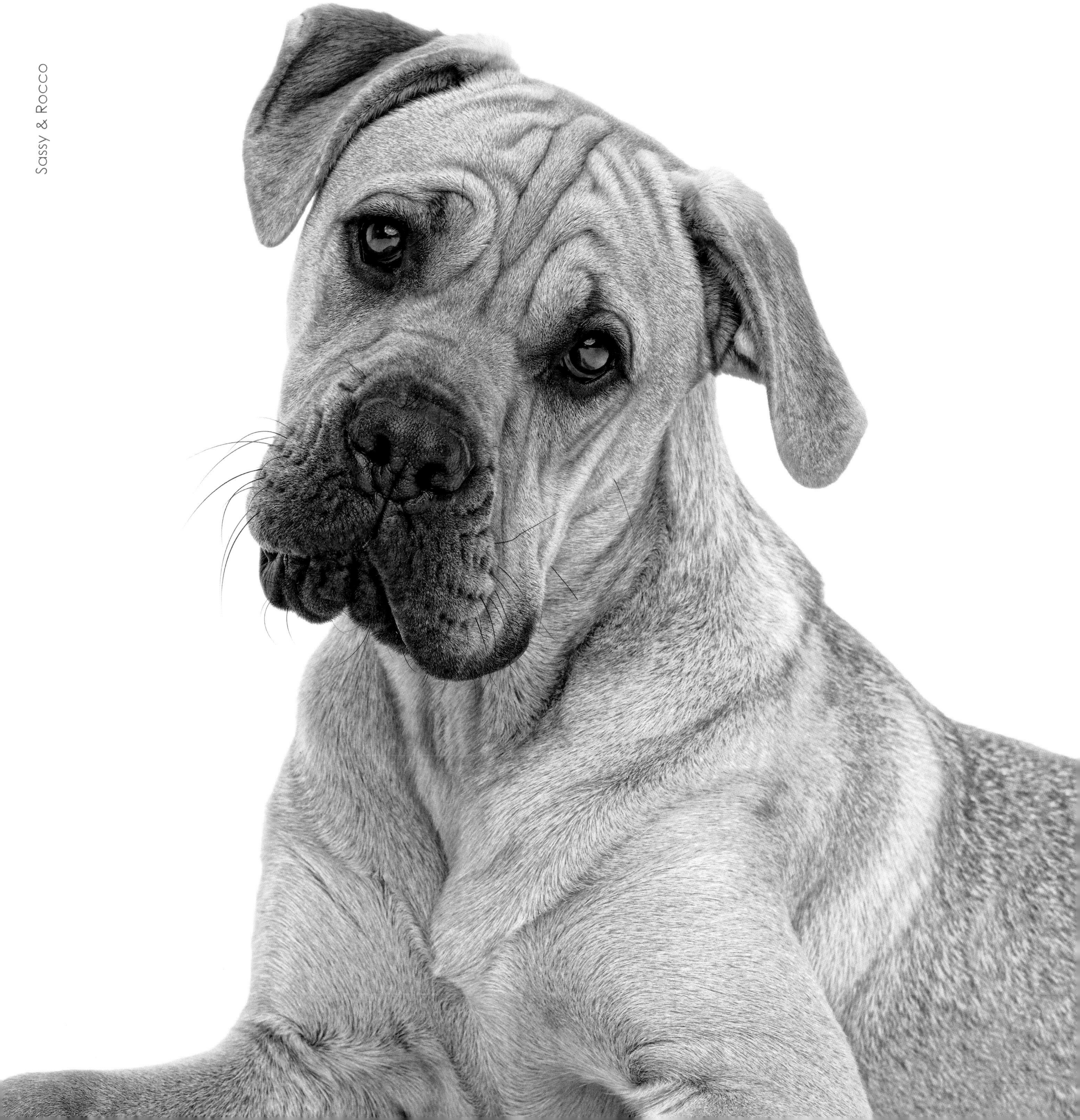

Sassy & Rocco

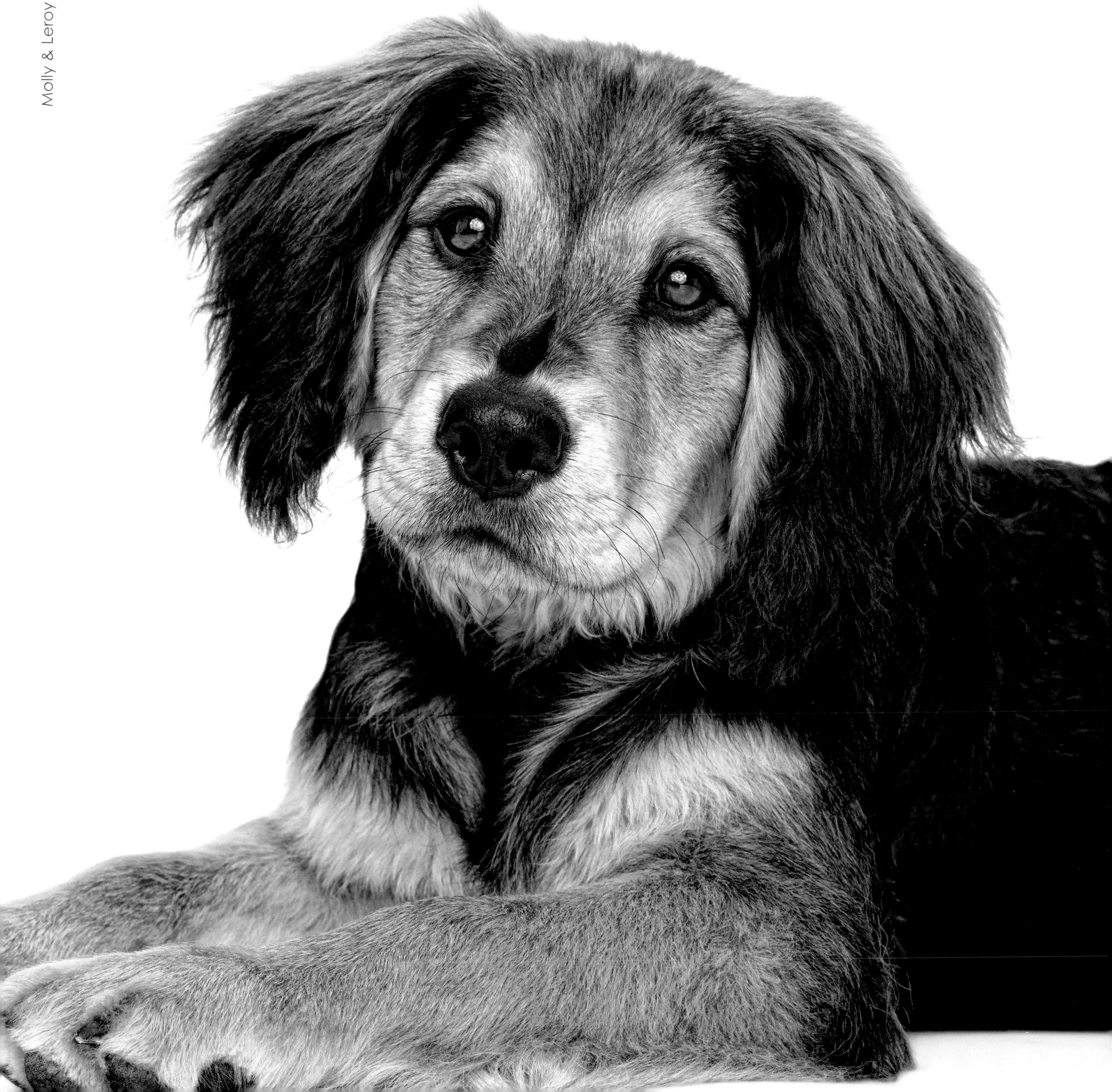

Molly & Leroy

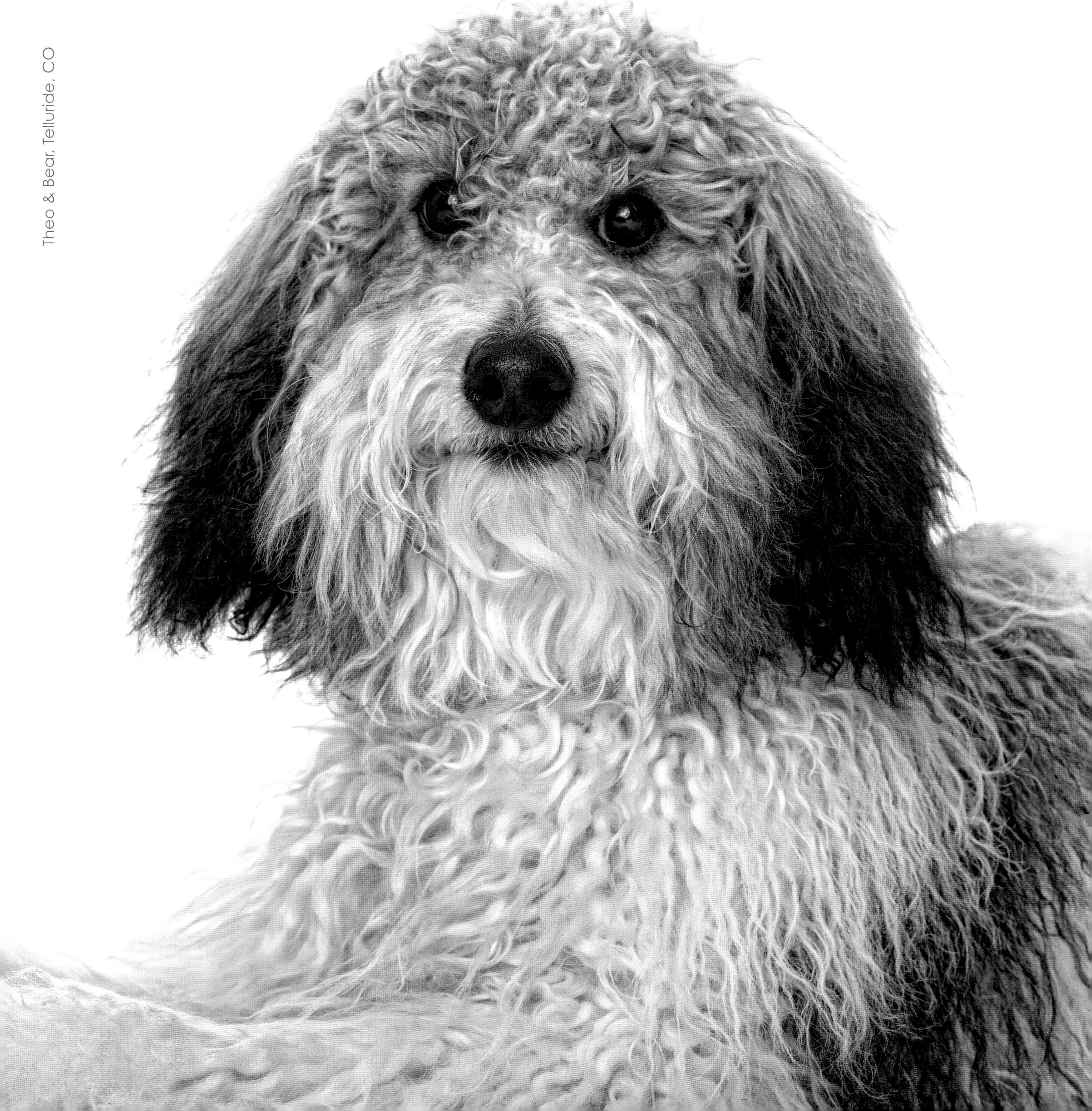

Theo & Bear, Telluride, CO

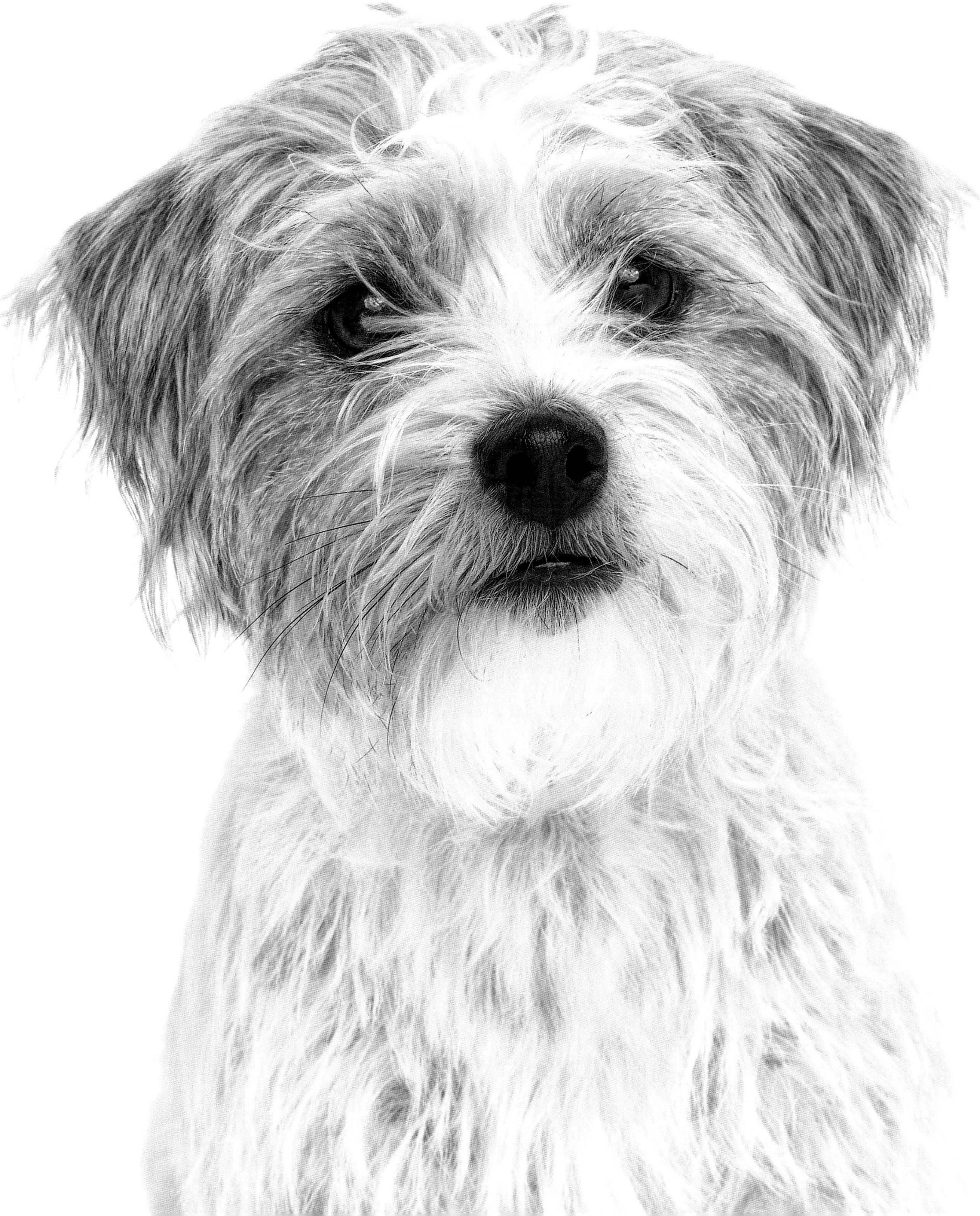
Scrutty & Daisy

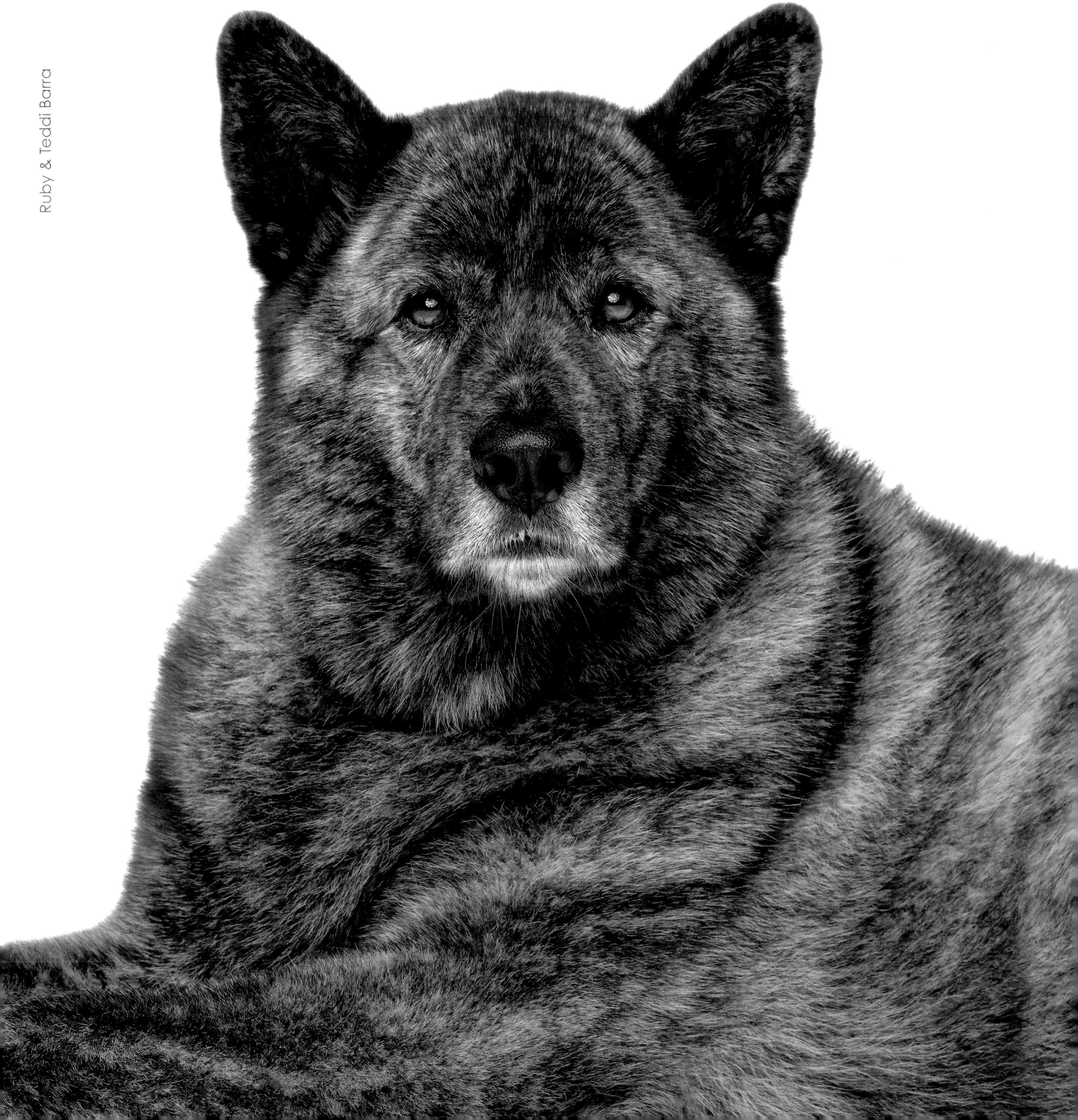

Ruby & Teddi Barra

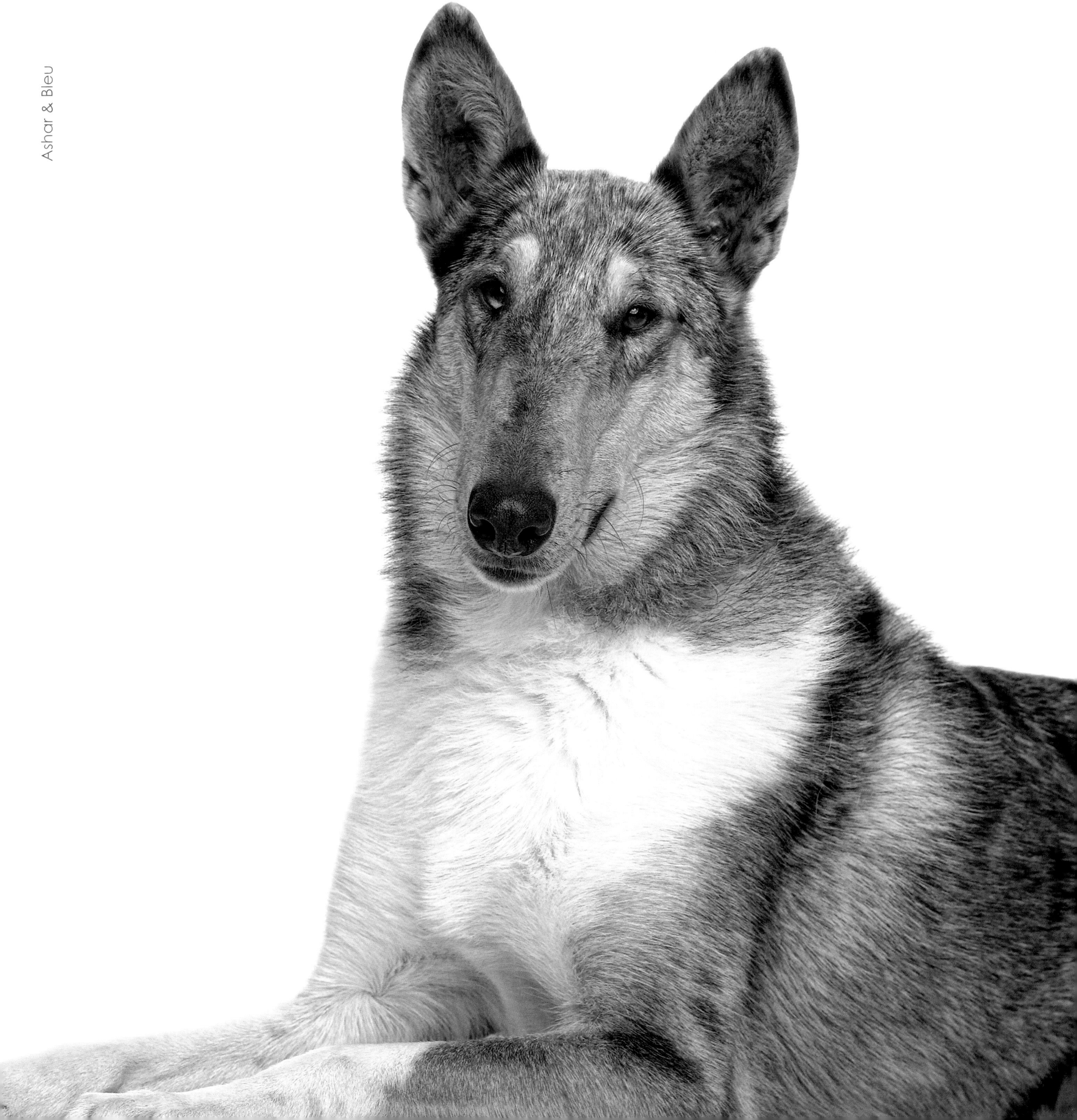

Ashar & Bleu

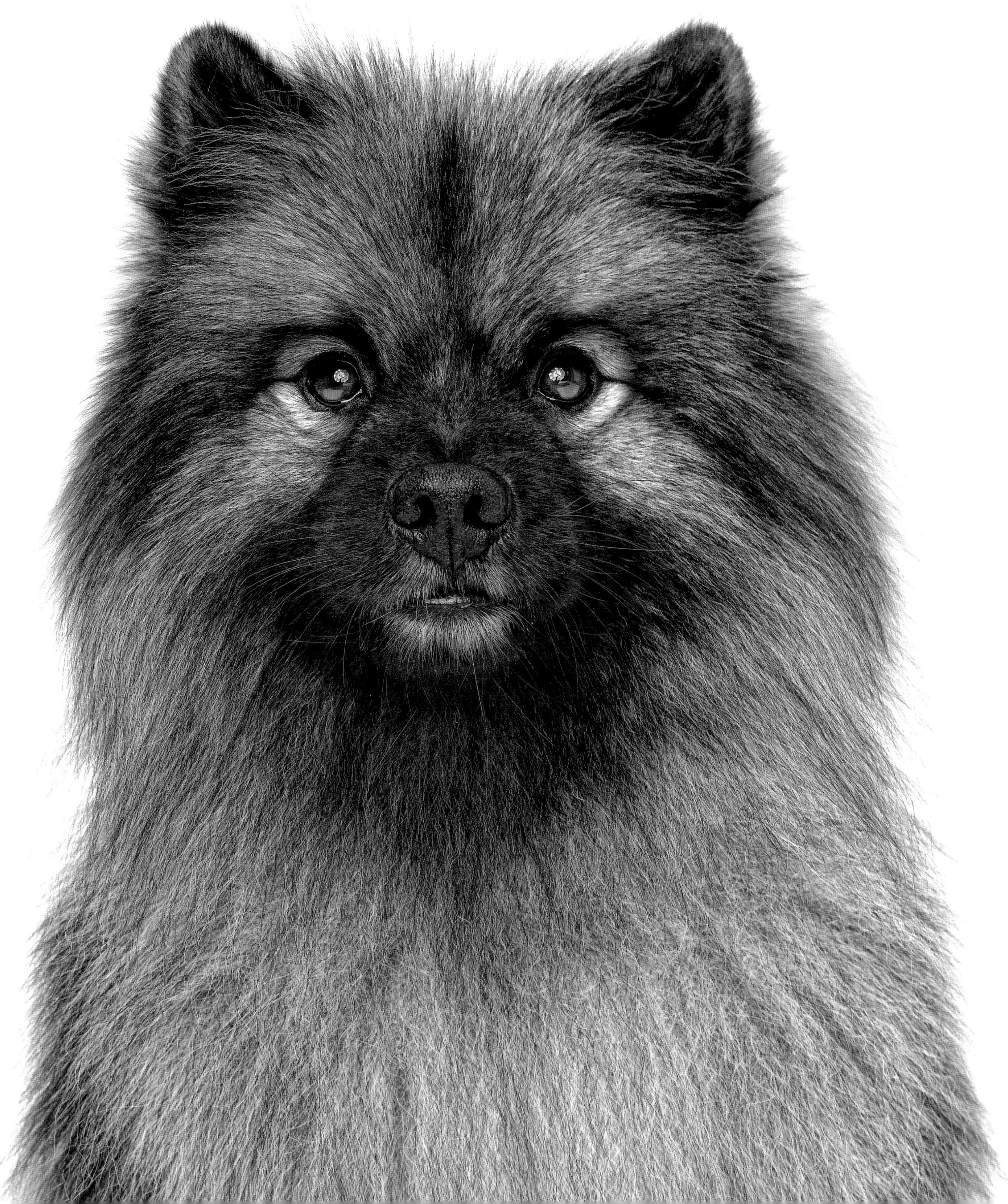

Isabella & Gus

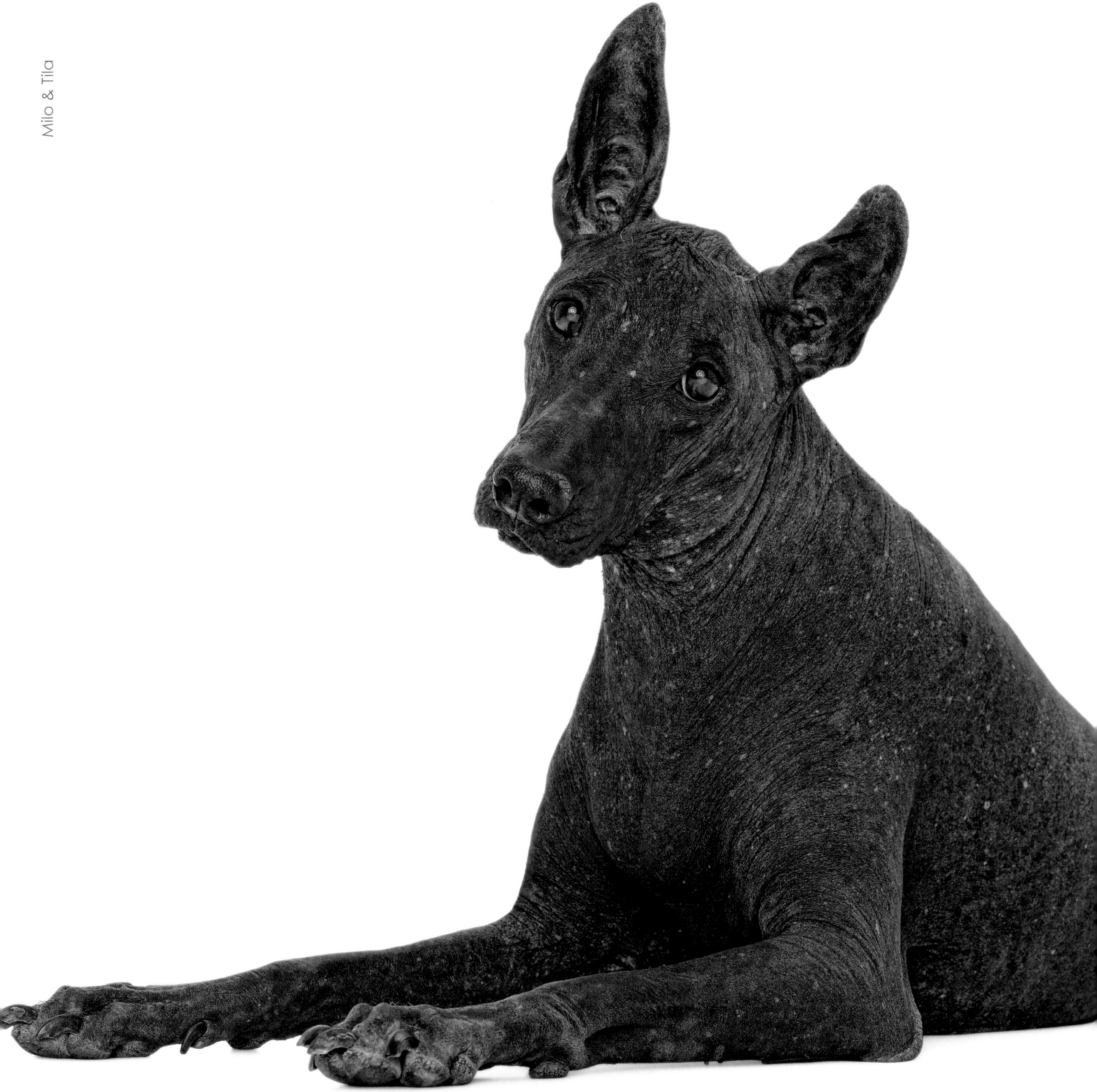

Milo & Tila

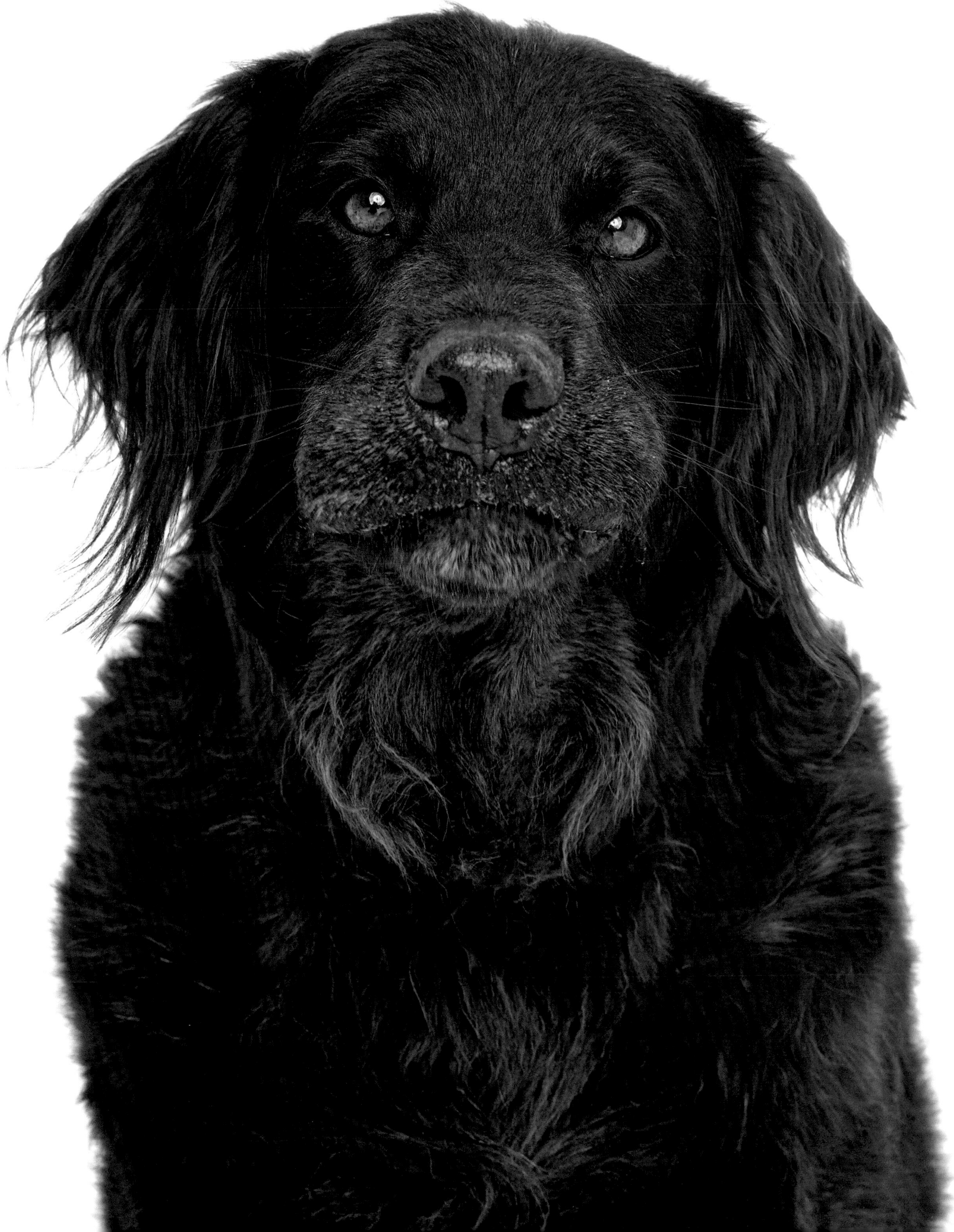

Homeless in 2013 & Homeless in 2012

Ash

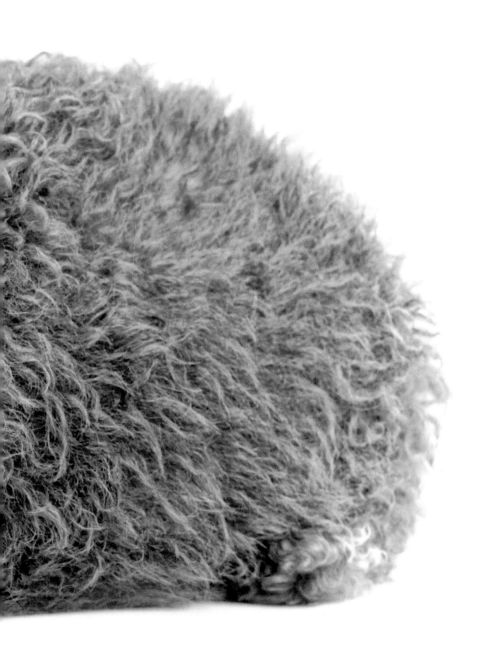

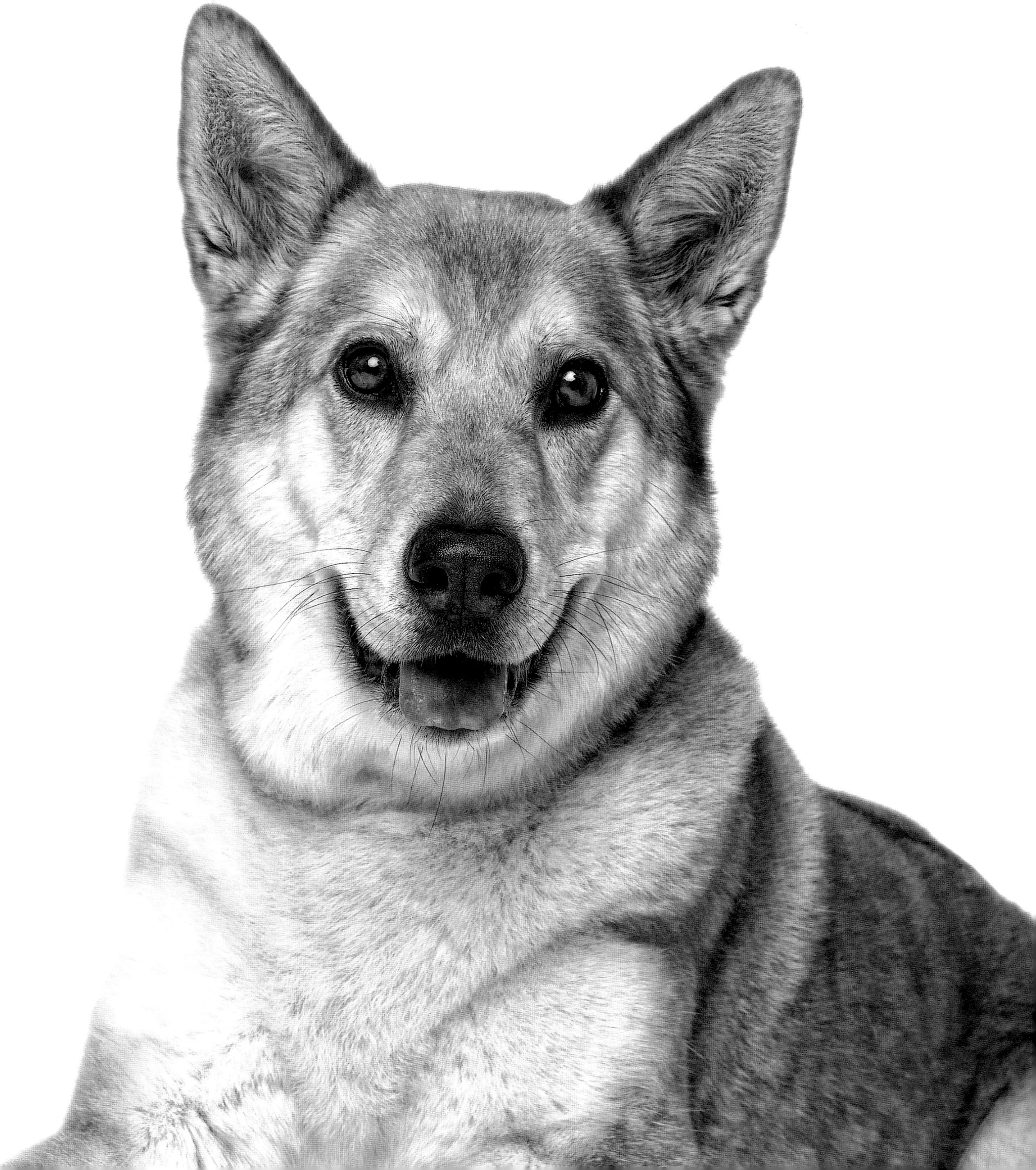

Takaio & Cole

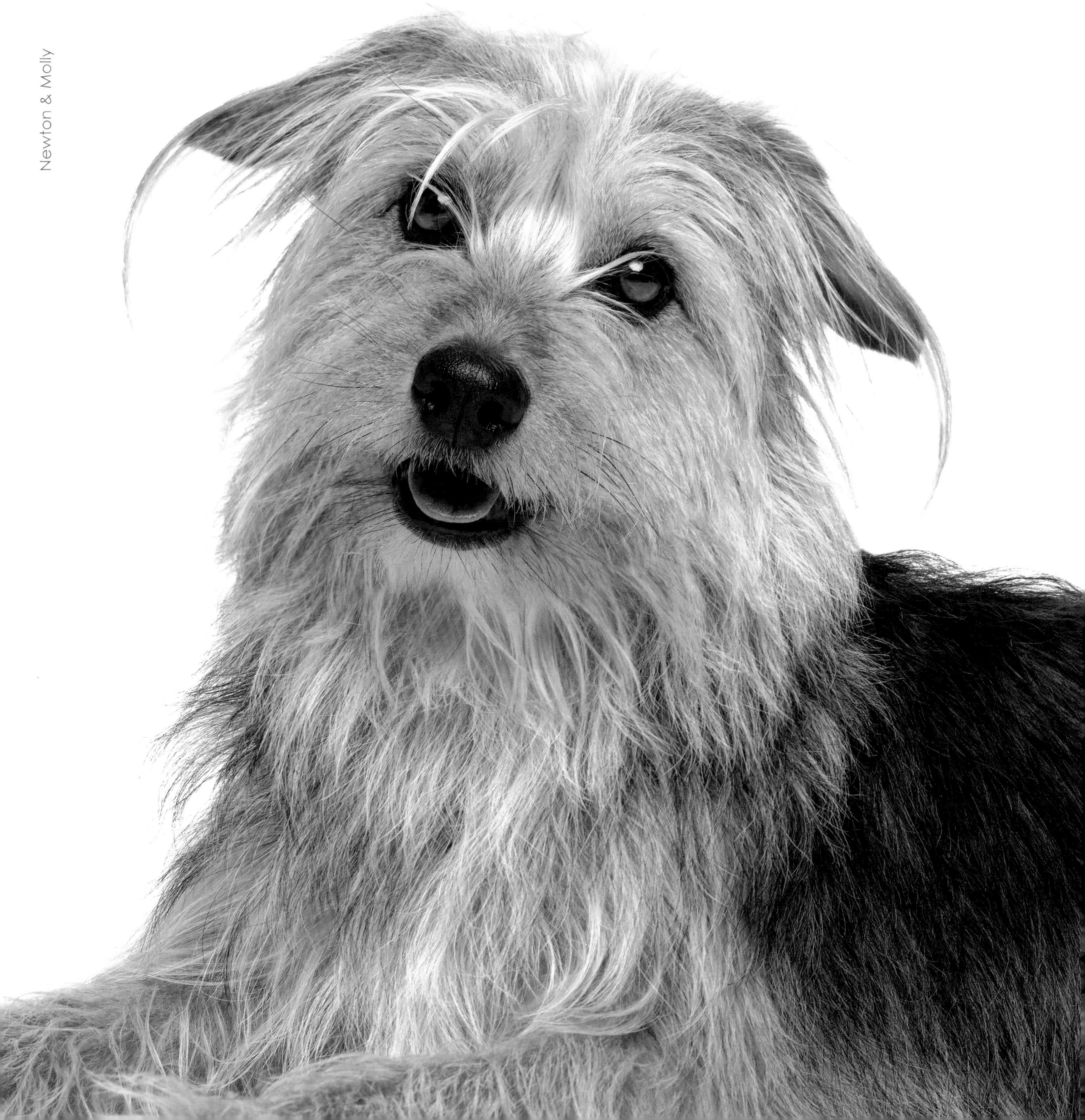

Newton & Molly

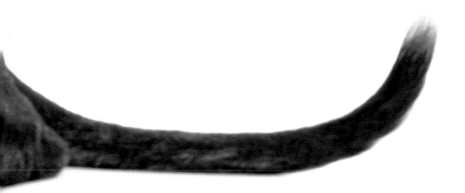

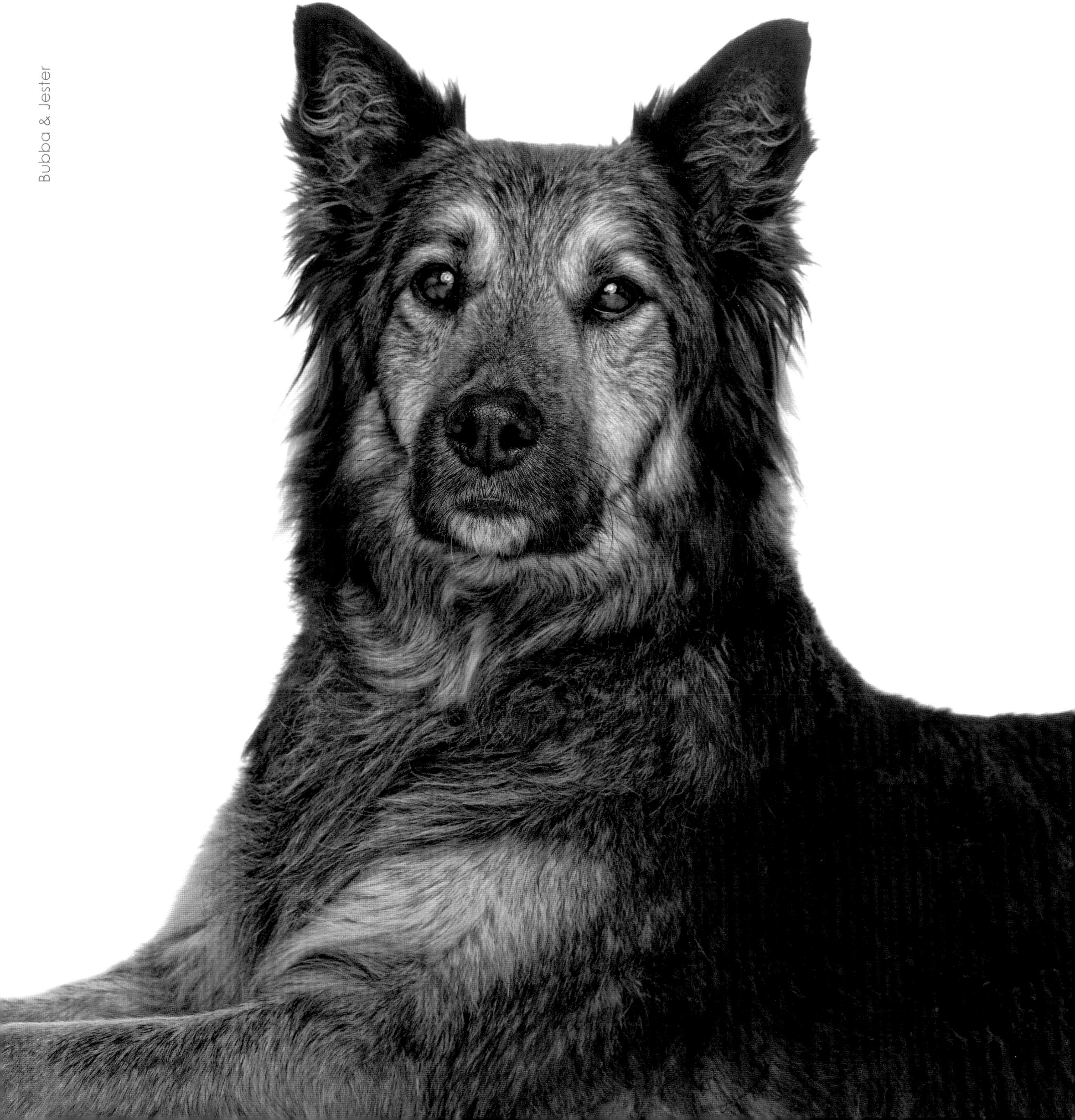

Bubba & Jester

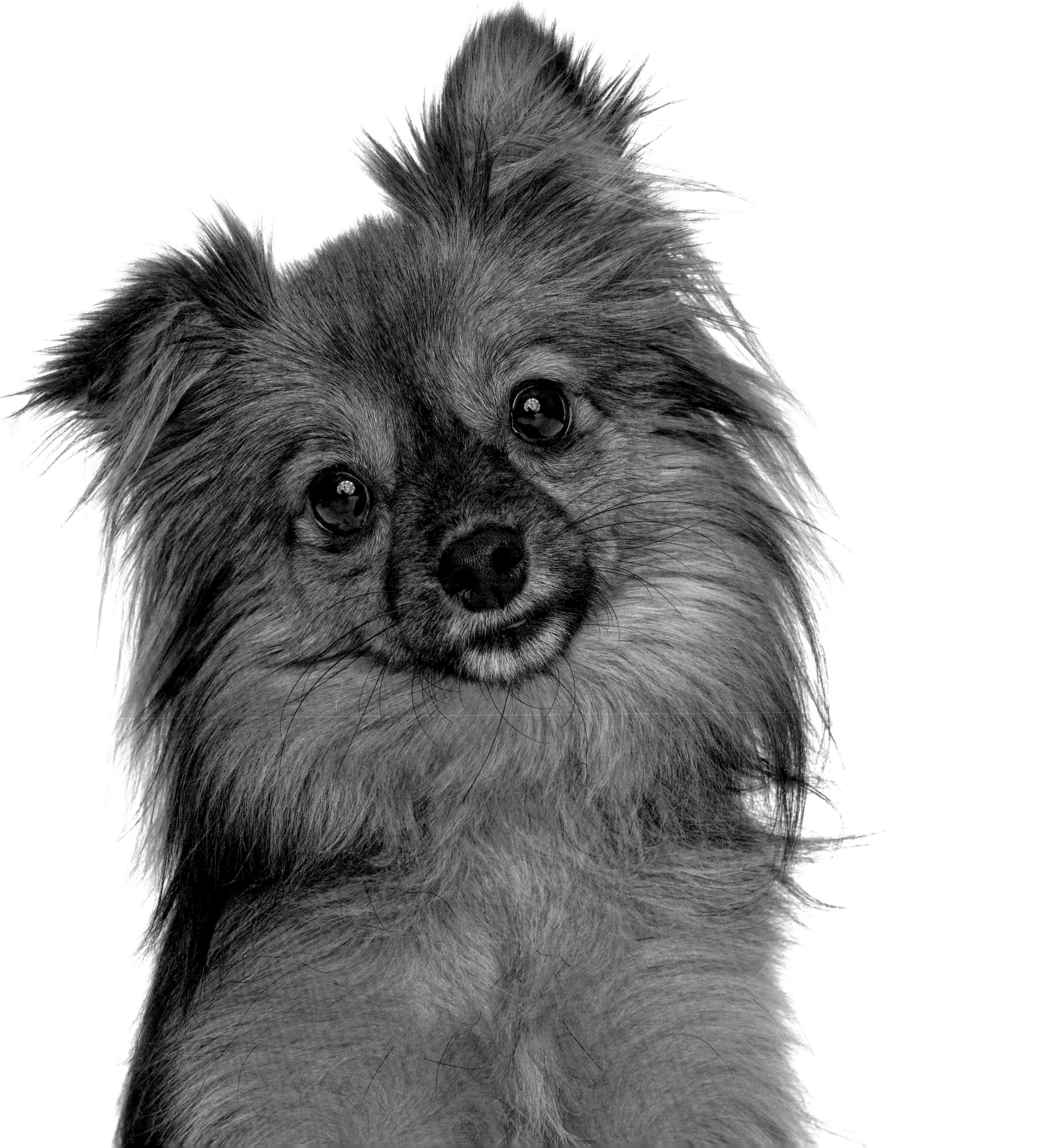

Zoey & Sparkles

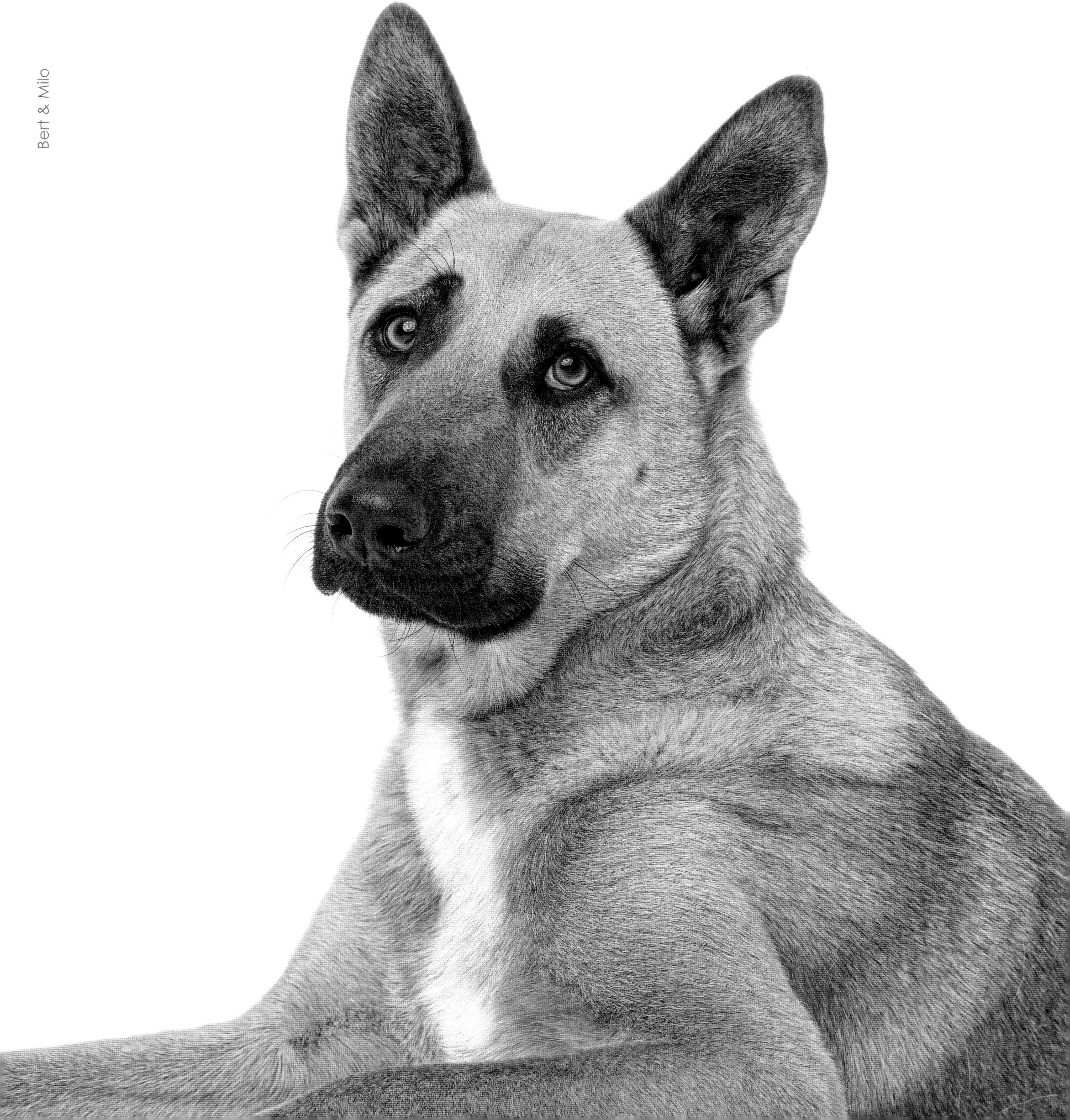

Bert & Milo

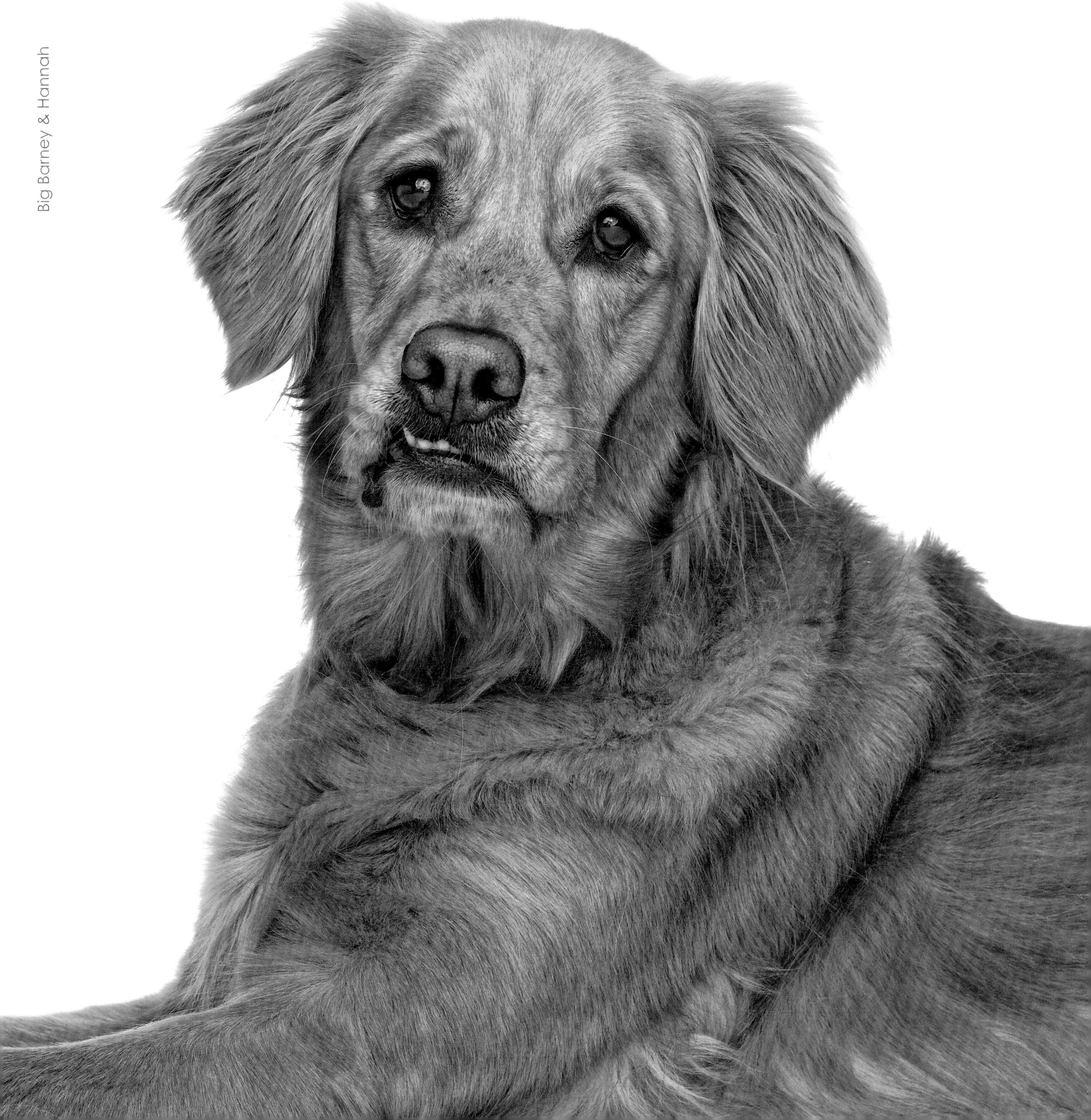

Big Barney & Hannah

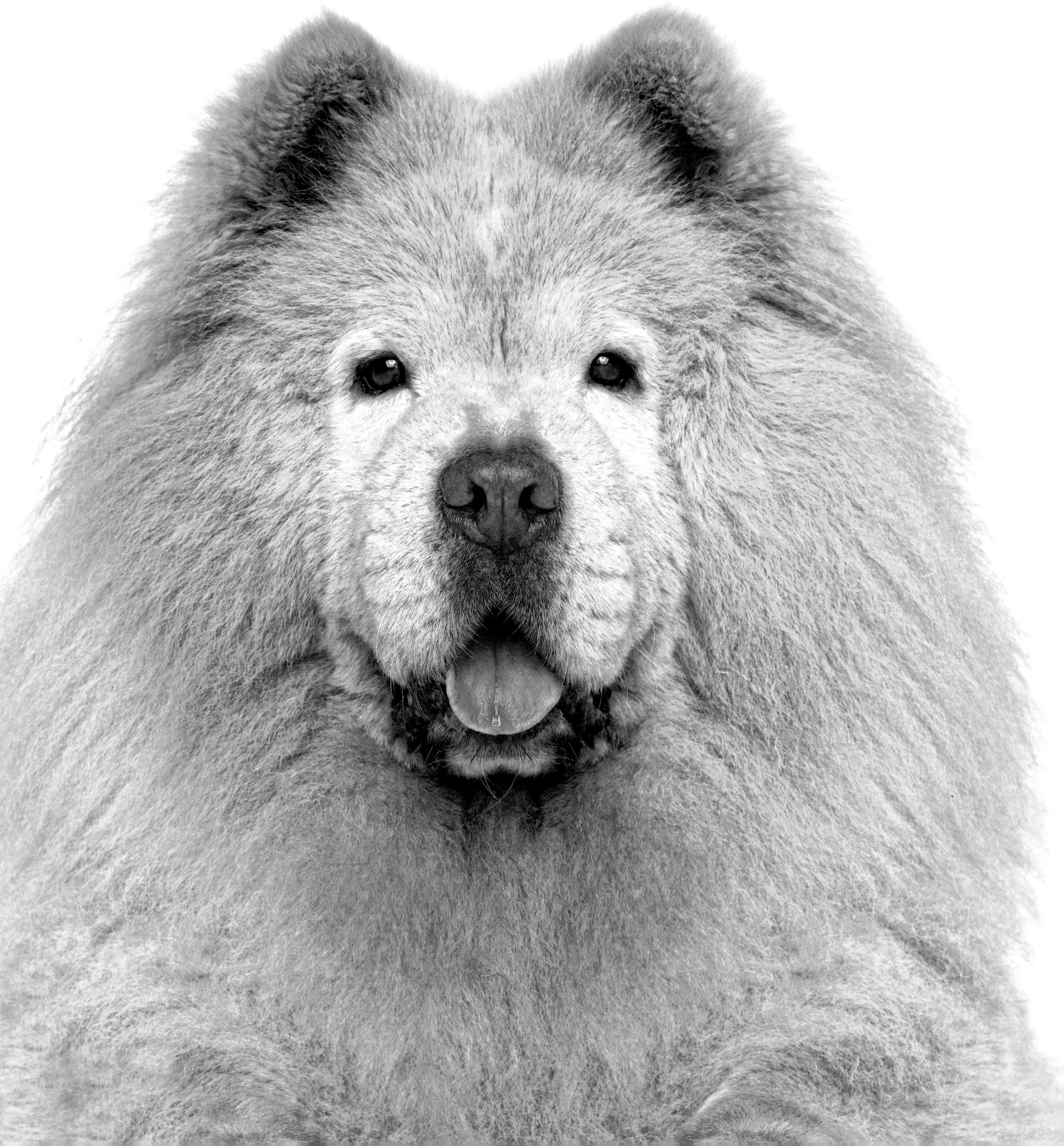

Phoebe & Sasha

Crissy & Vinny

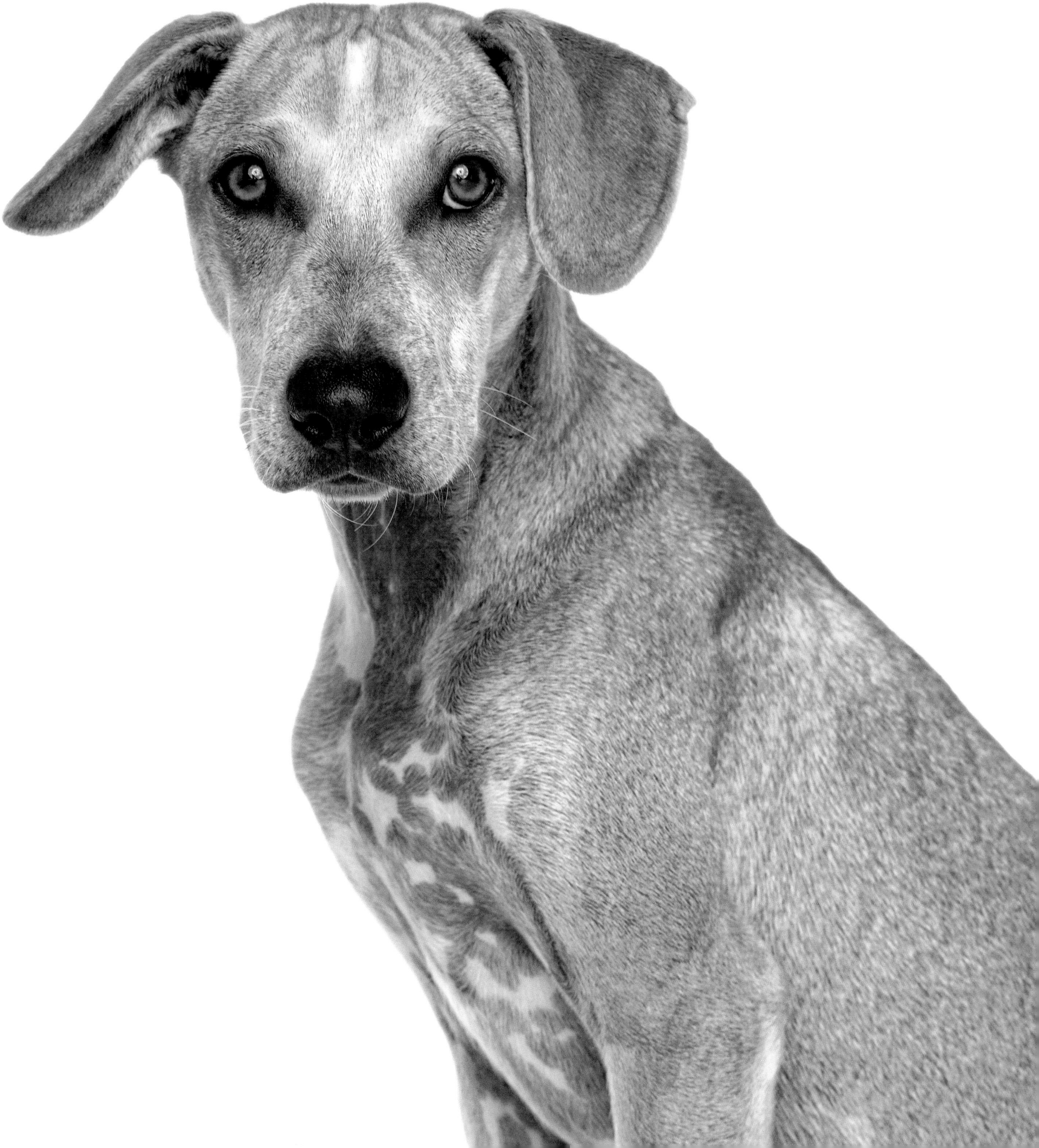

Gulliver & Kona

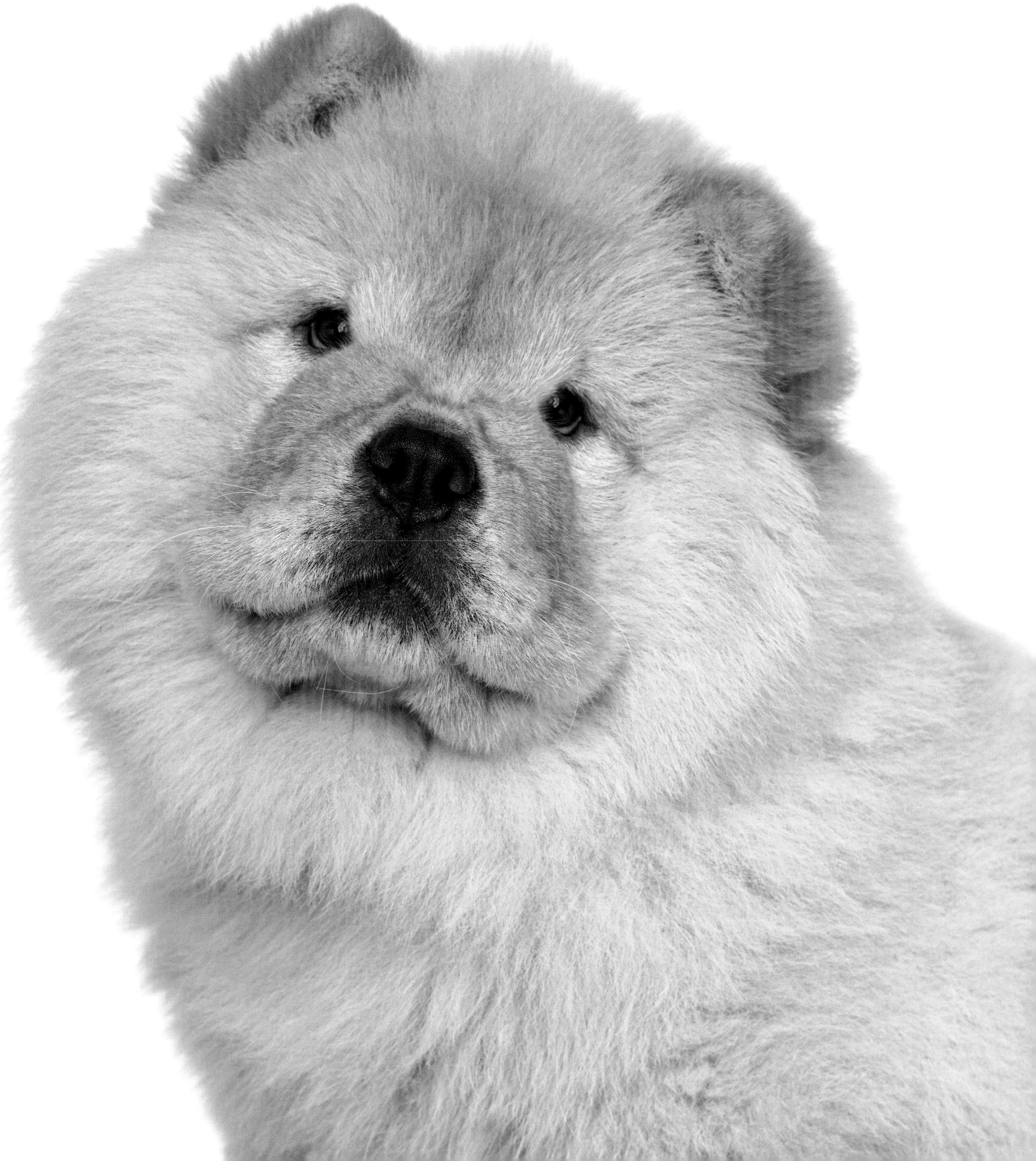

Ramsey & Chia

Lily & Tony

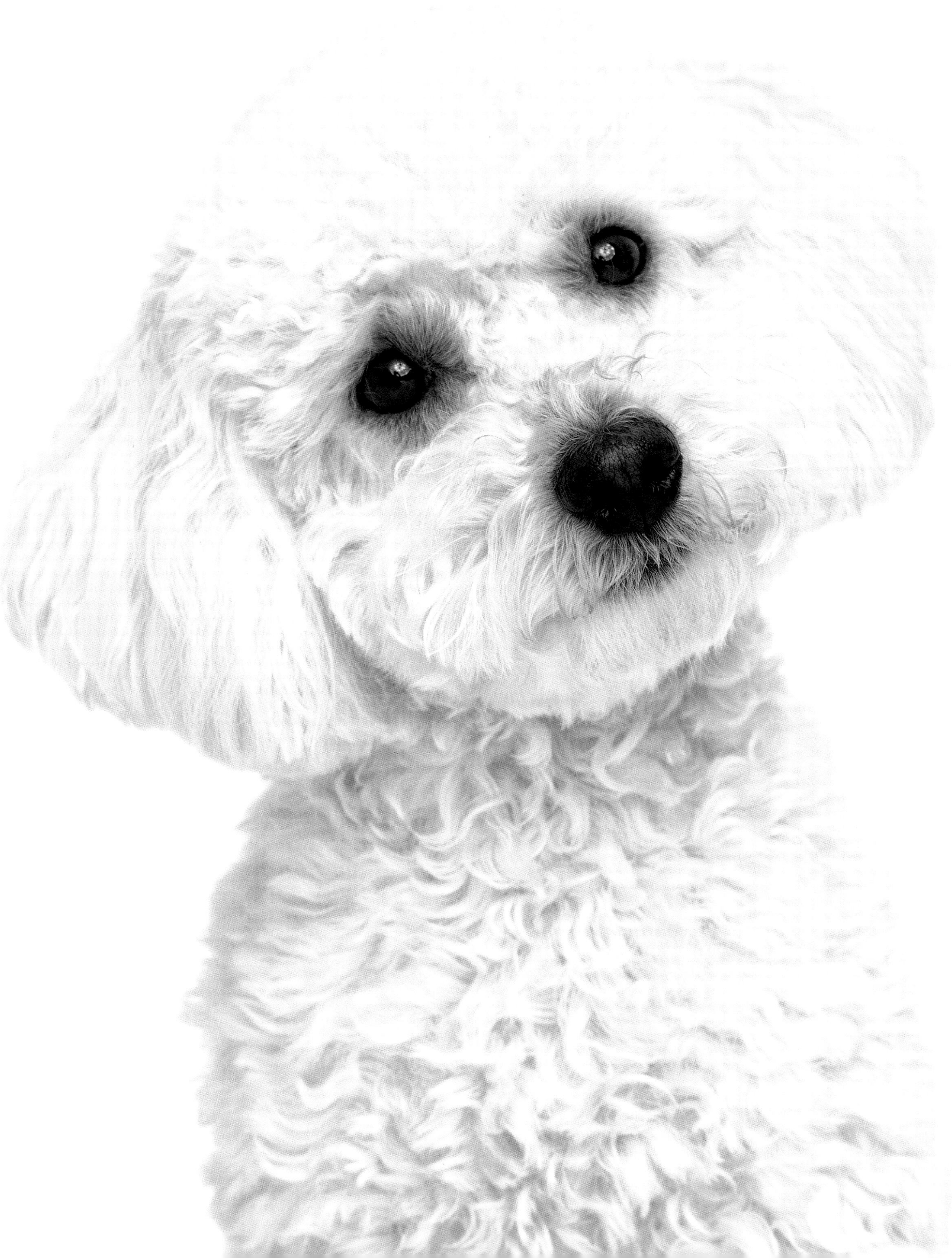

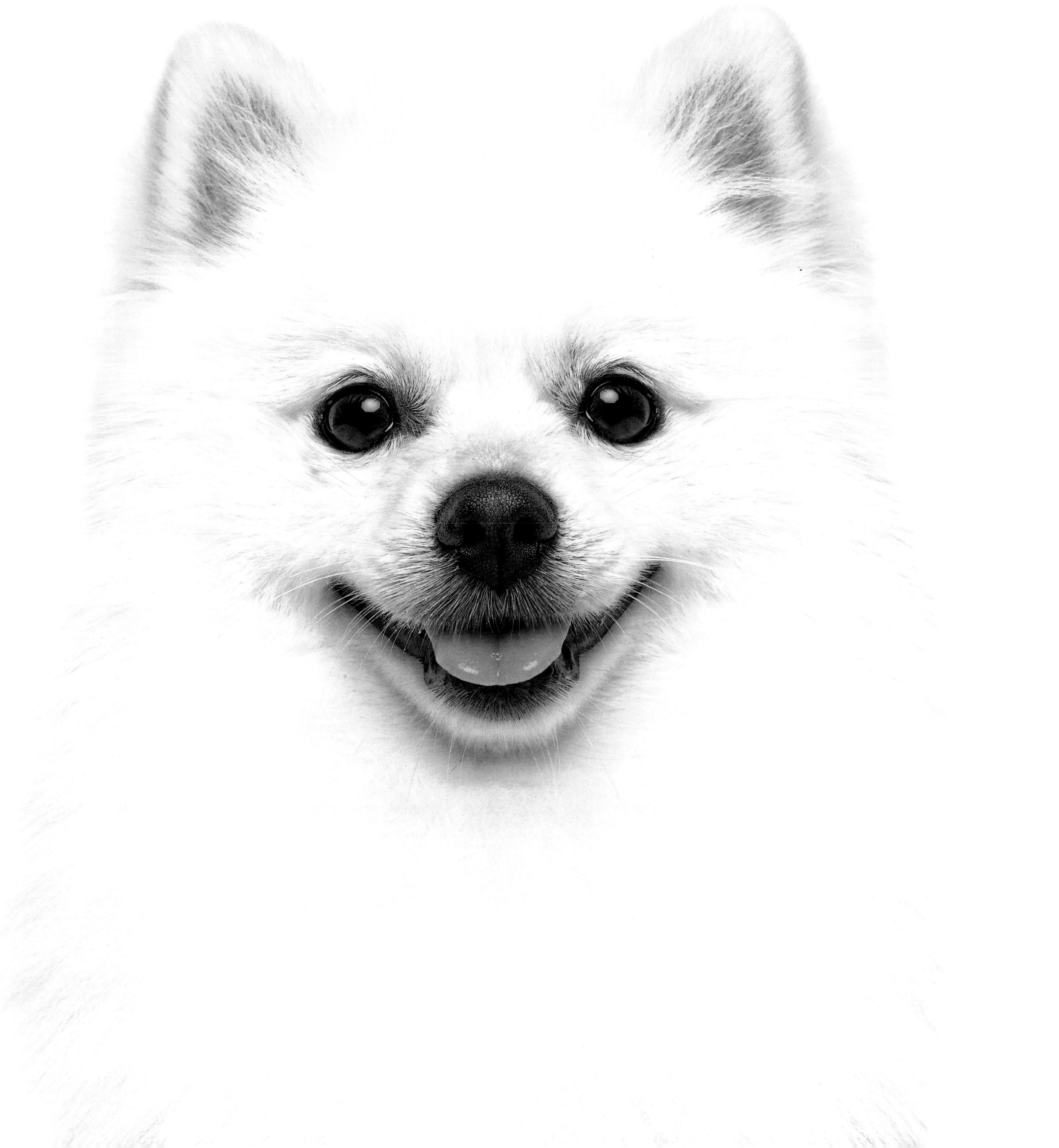

Daisy & Napoleon

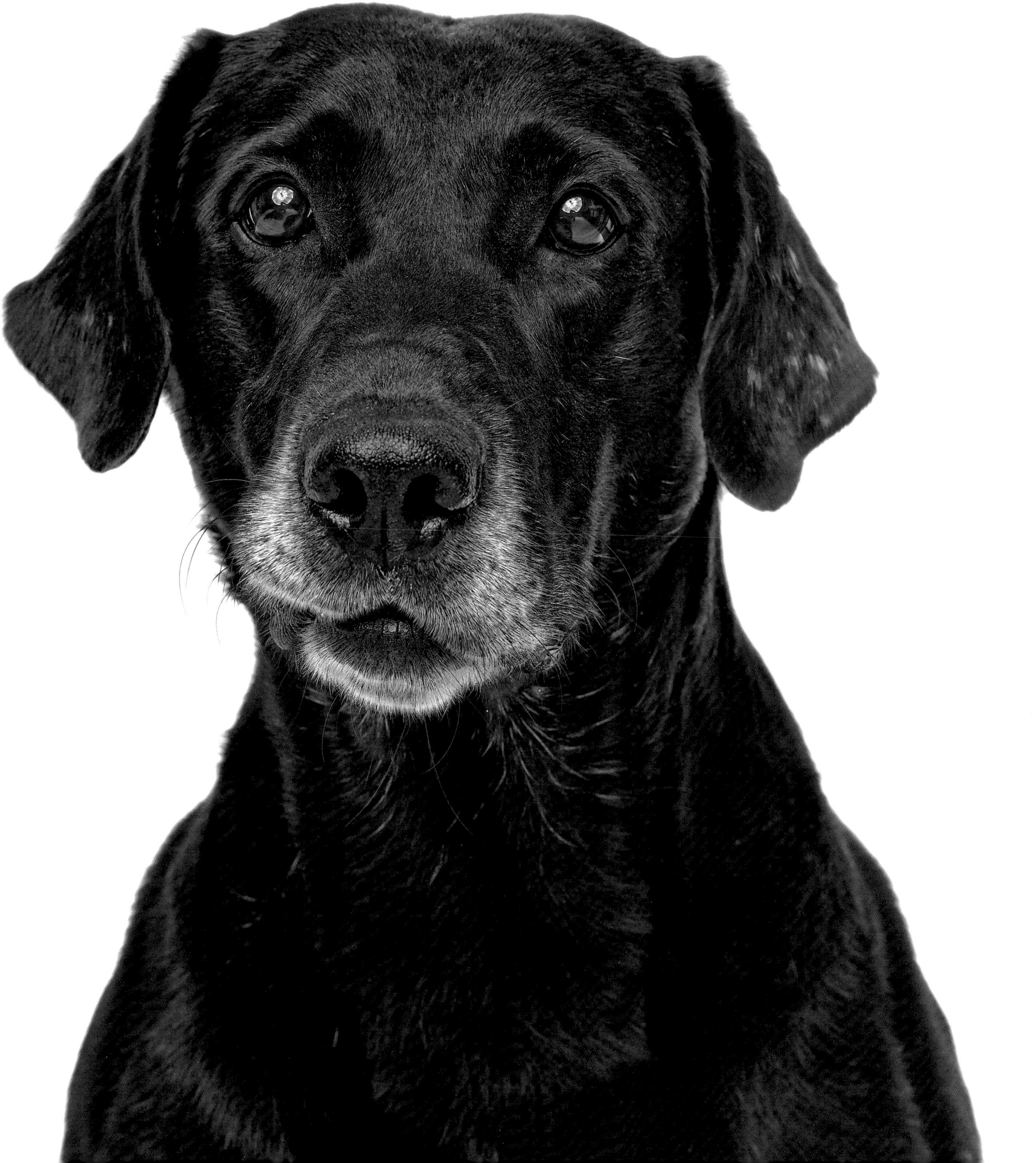

Badger & Bleu

Ernie & Bochy

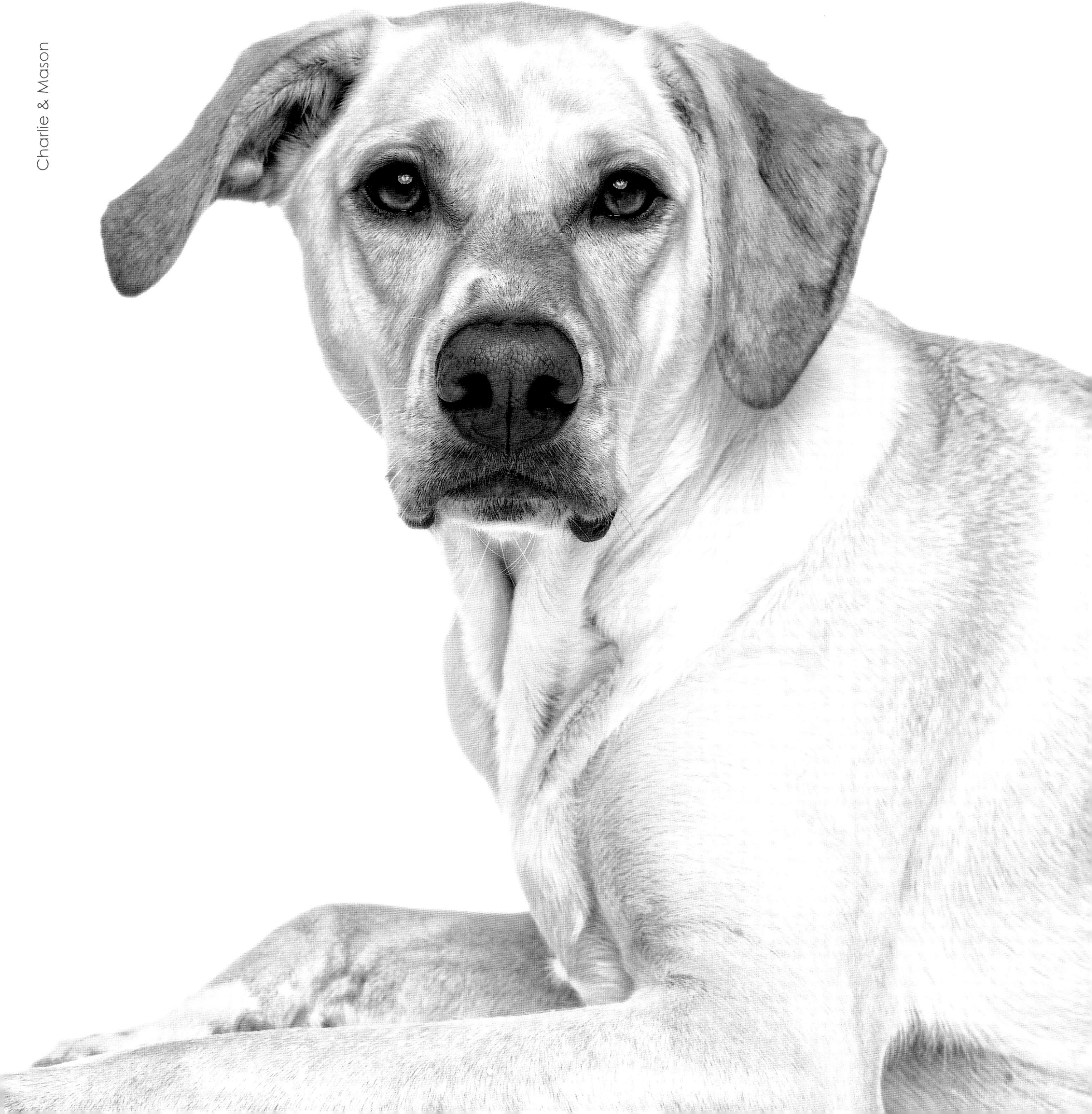

Charlie & Mason

Duke & Layla

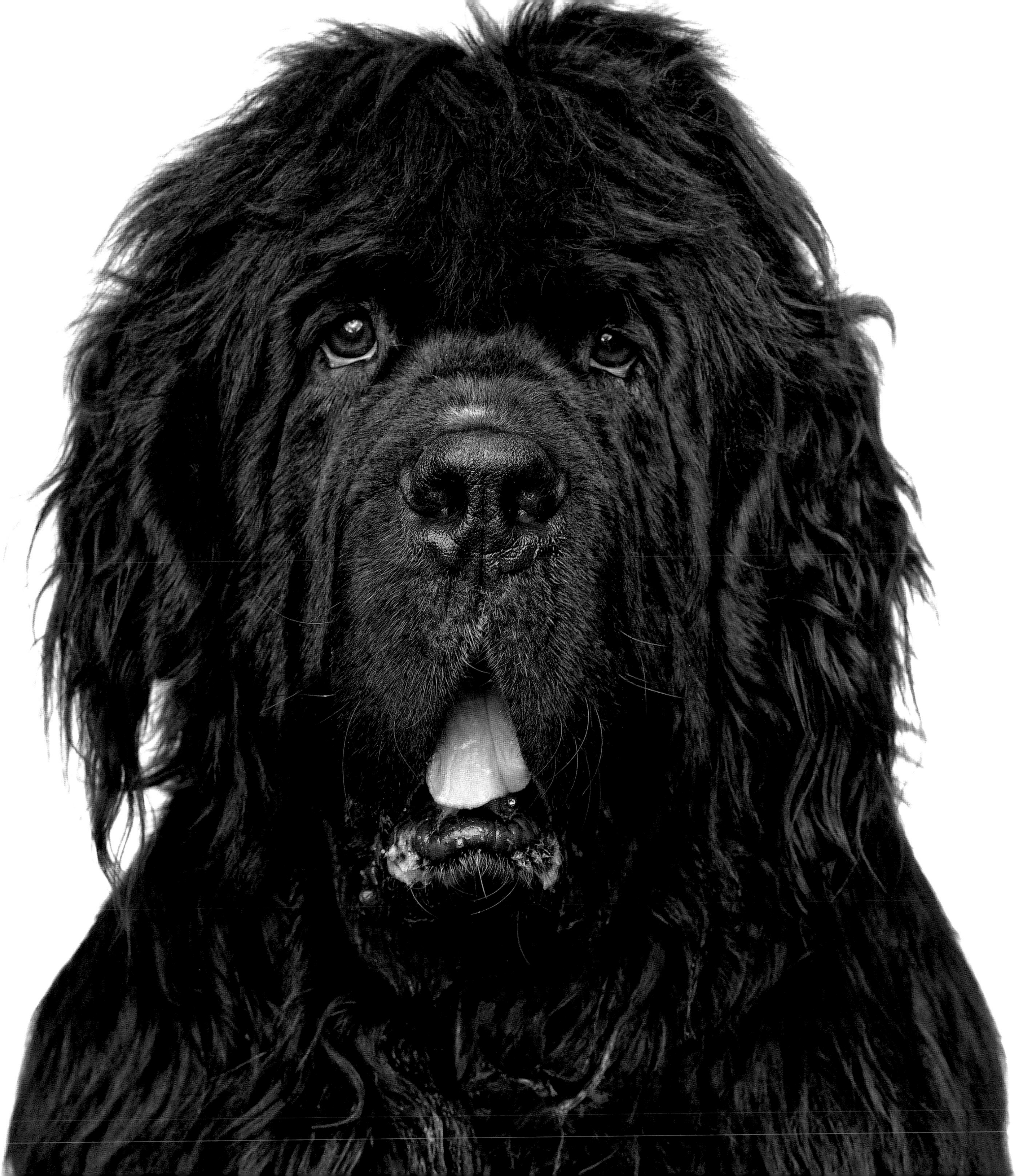

Apollo & Atlas

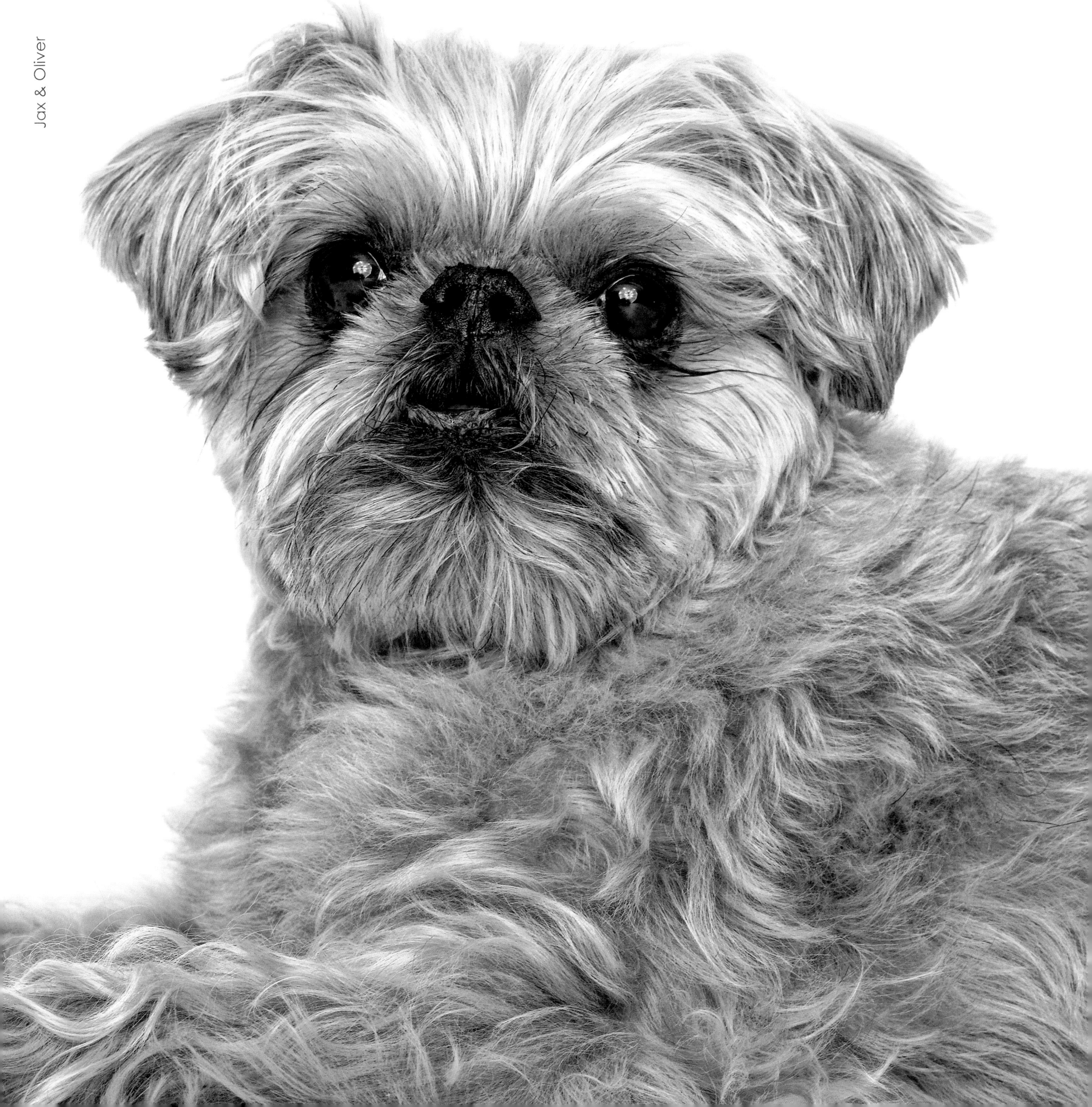

Jax & Oliver

Jag & Charlie

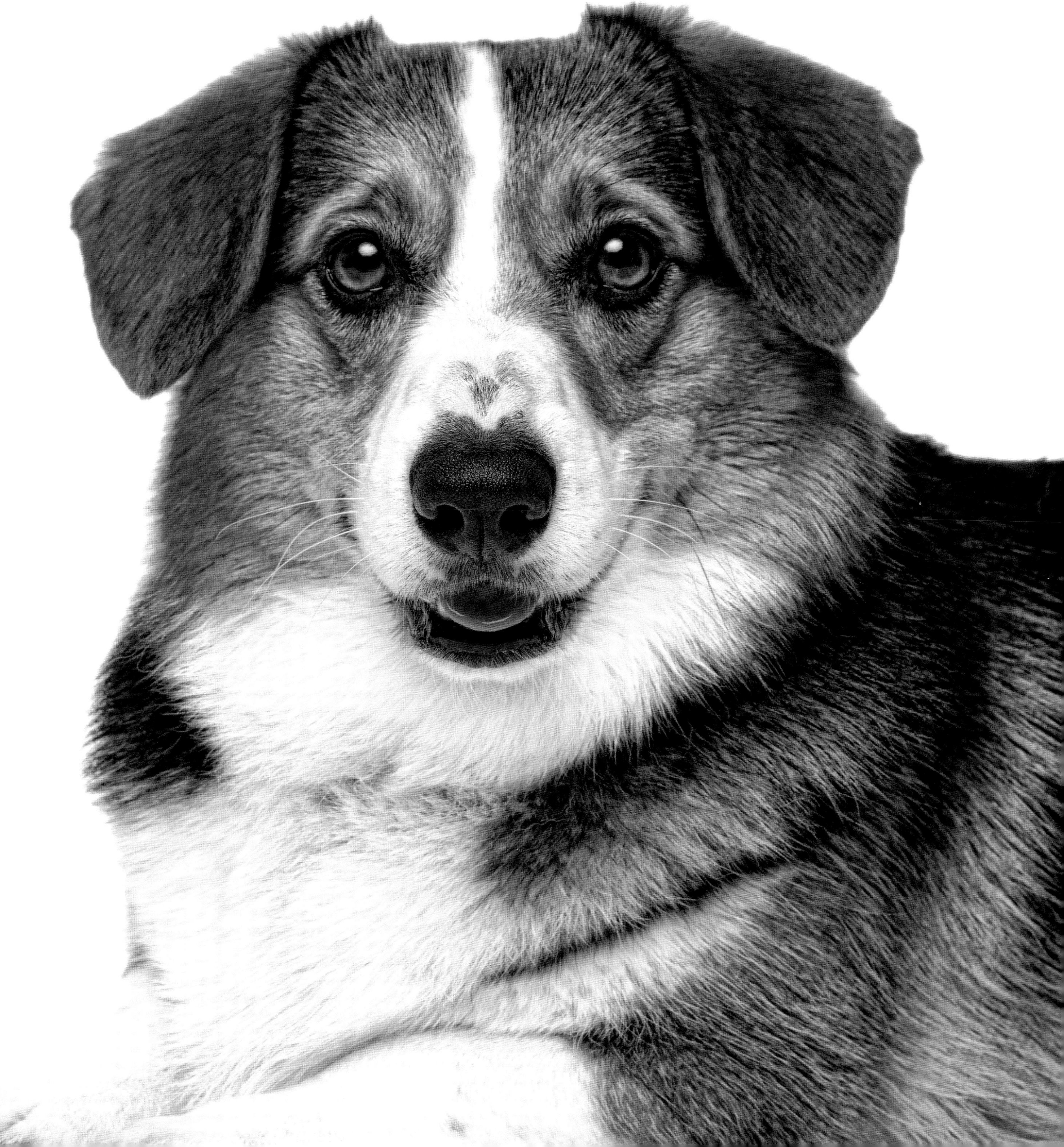

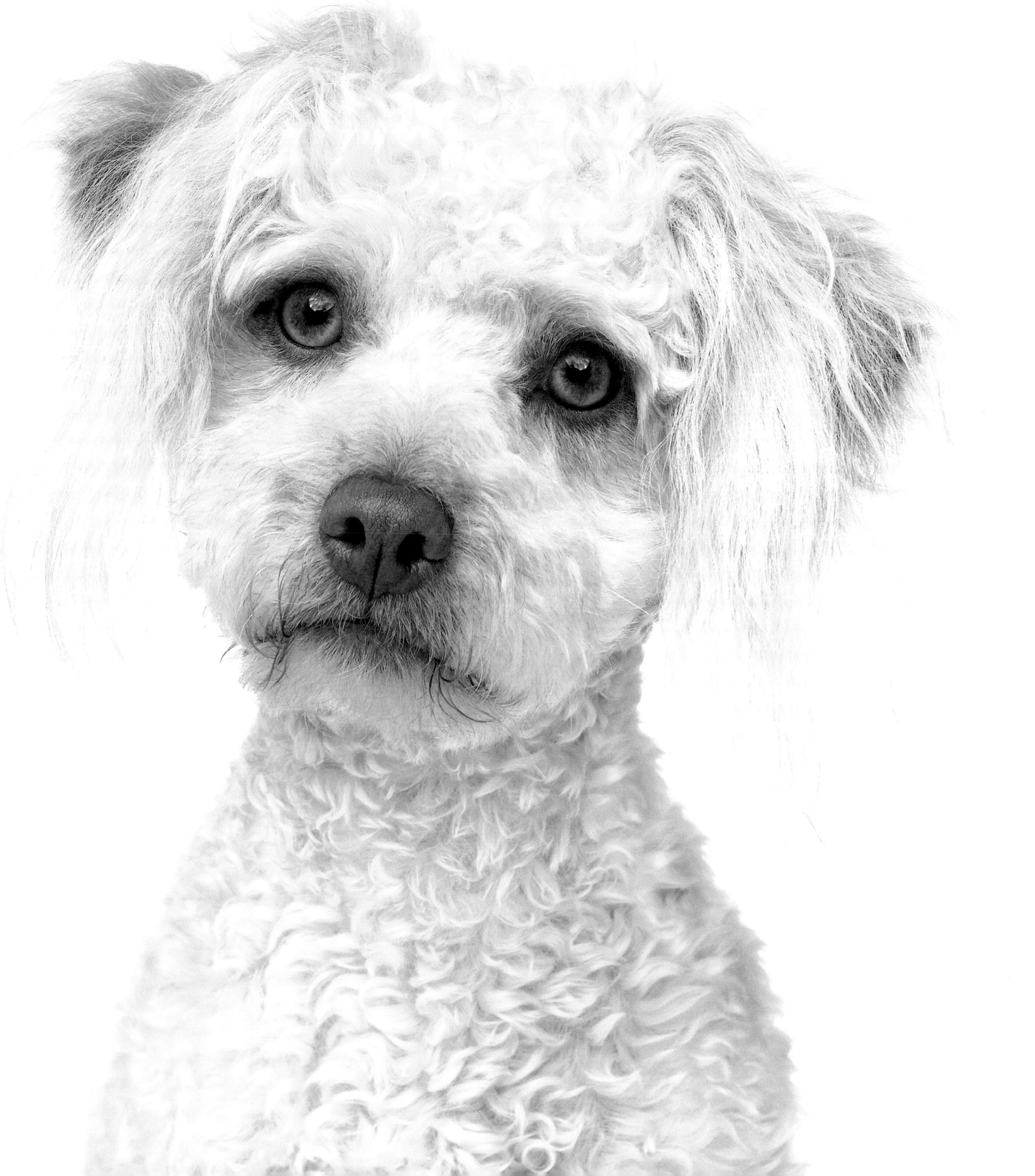

Blast & Sid

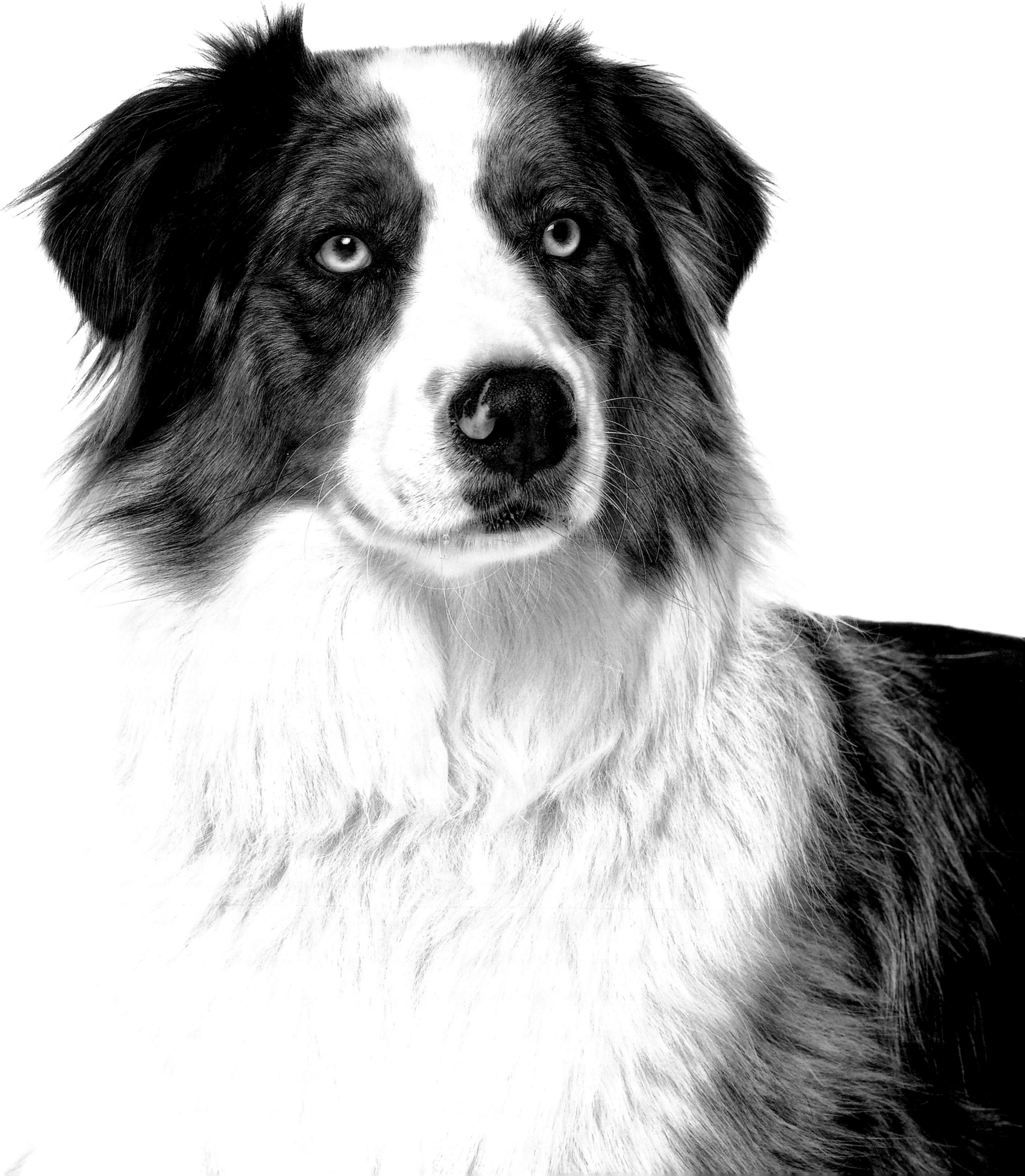

Cooper & Ozzy

Maisie

Bogey

Jamie Moon & Emily

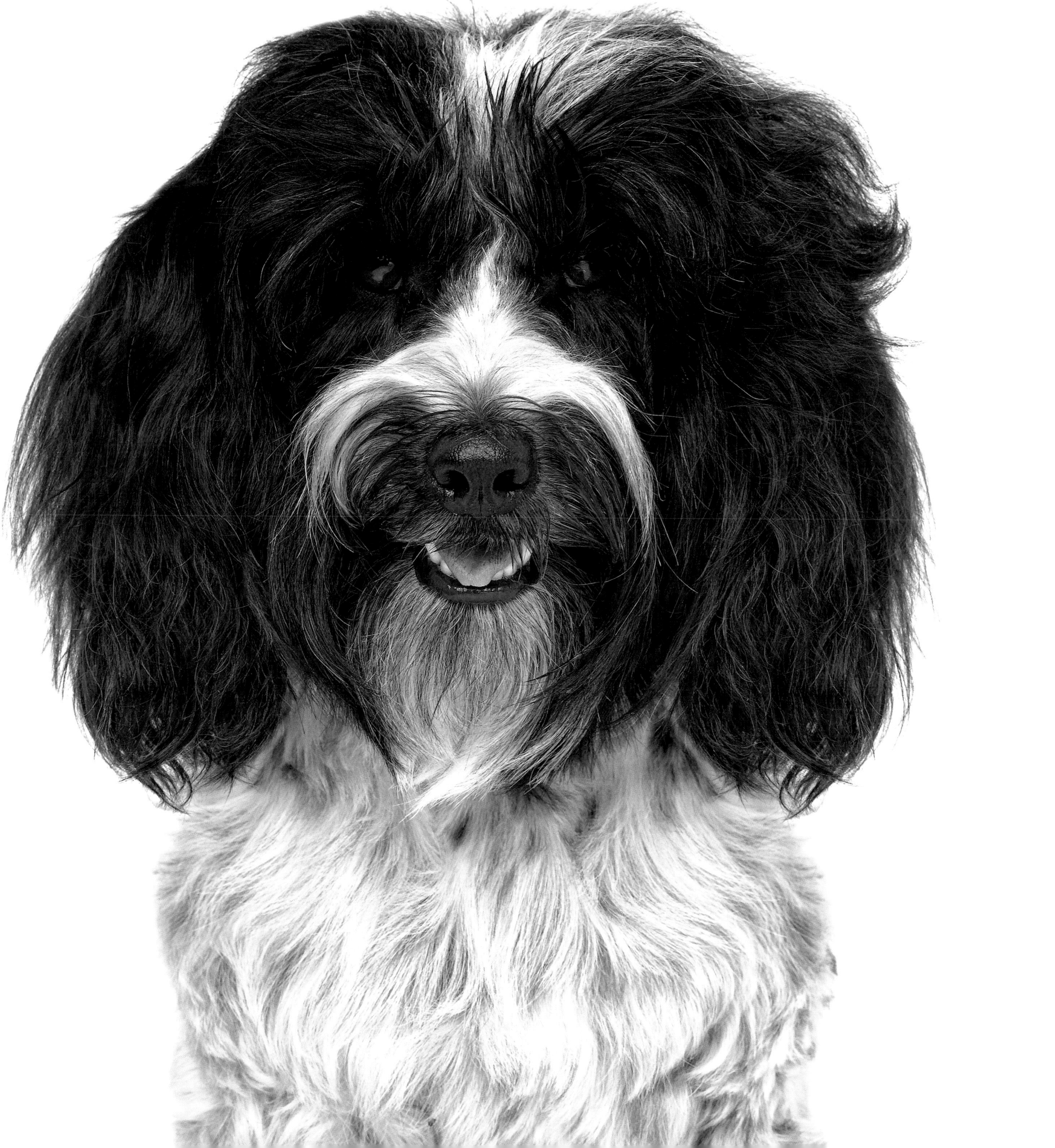

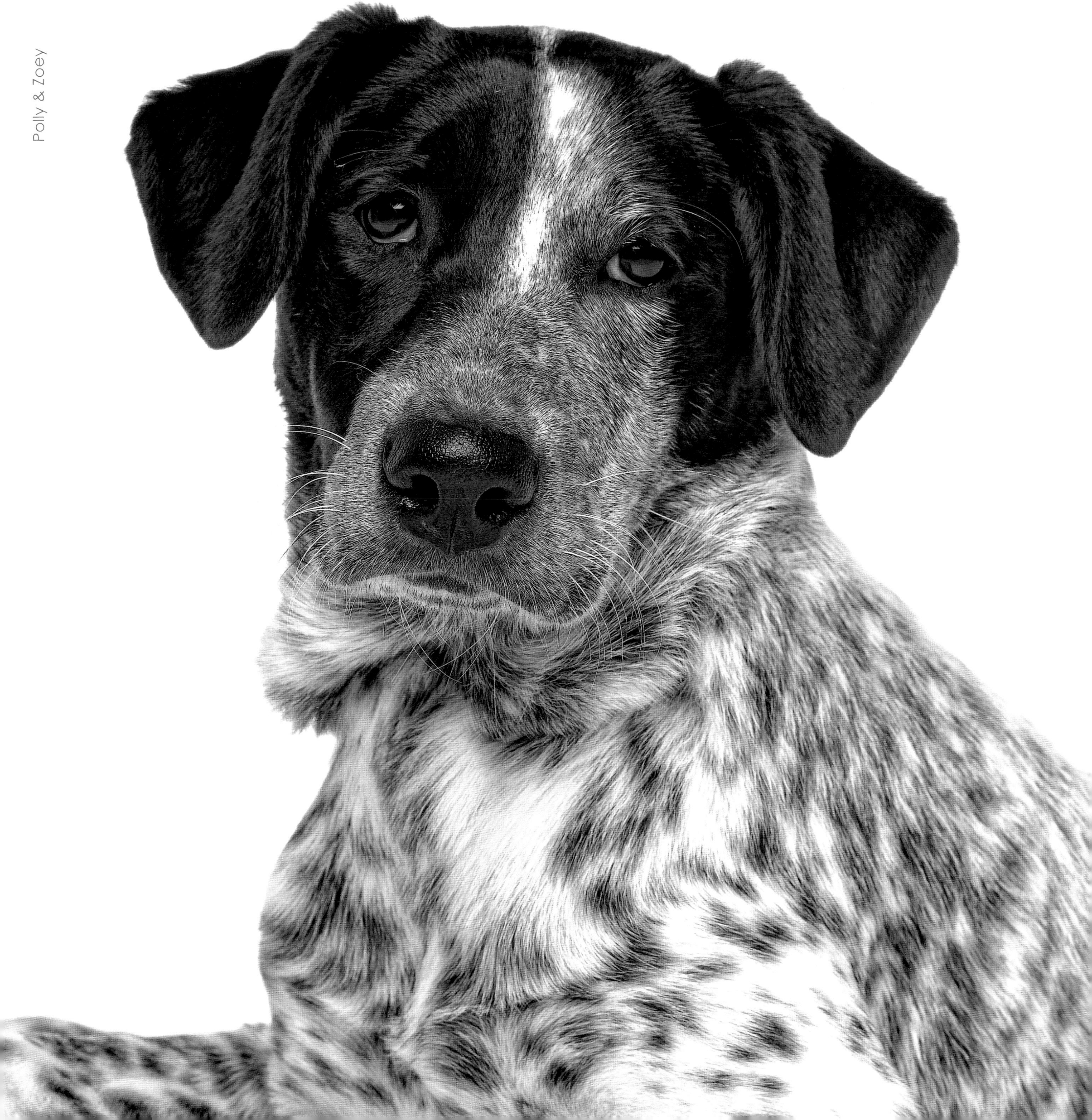

Polly & Zoey

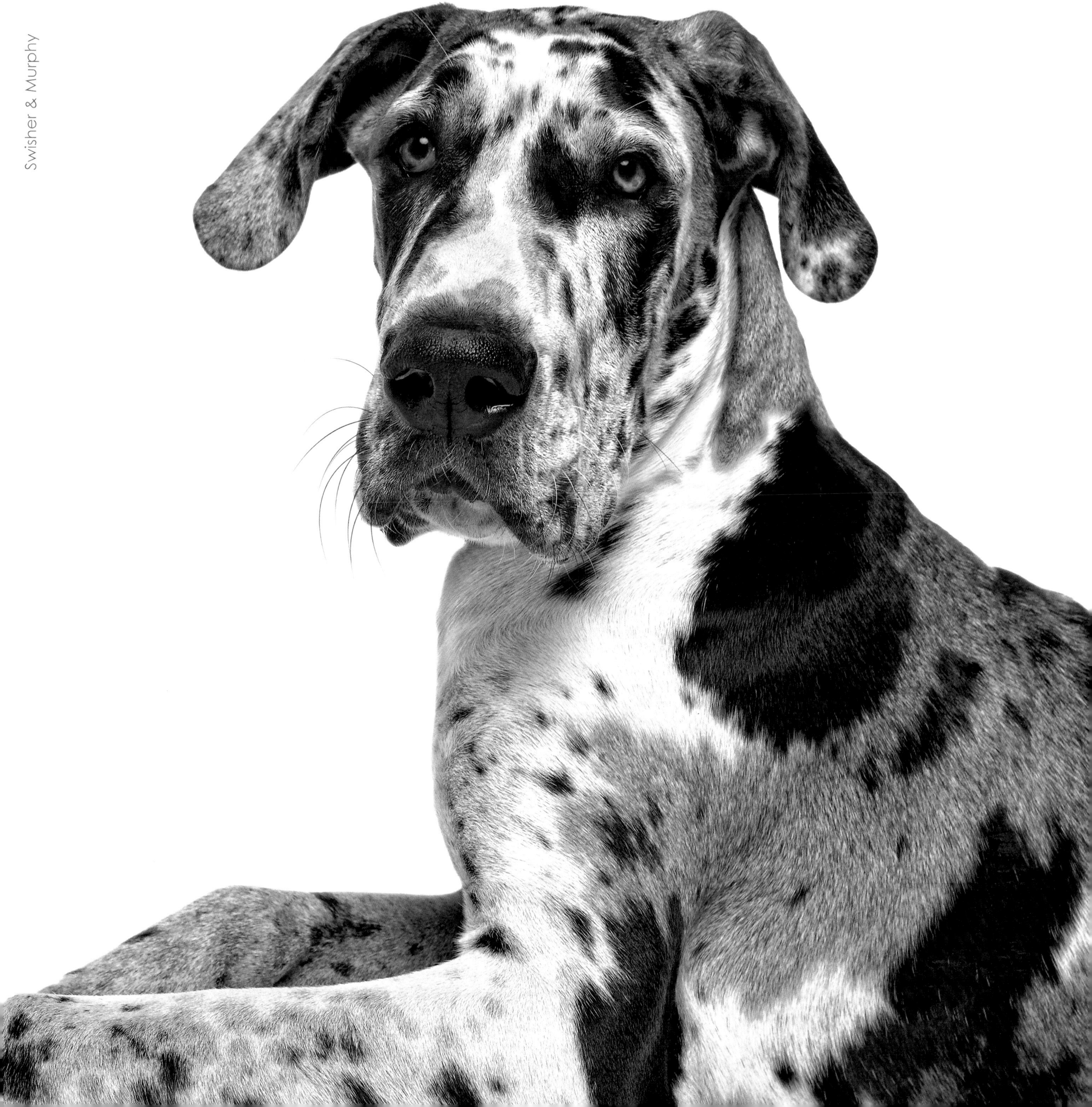
Swisher & Murphy

Gaby & Suzie Q

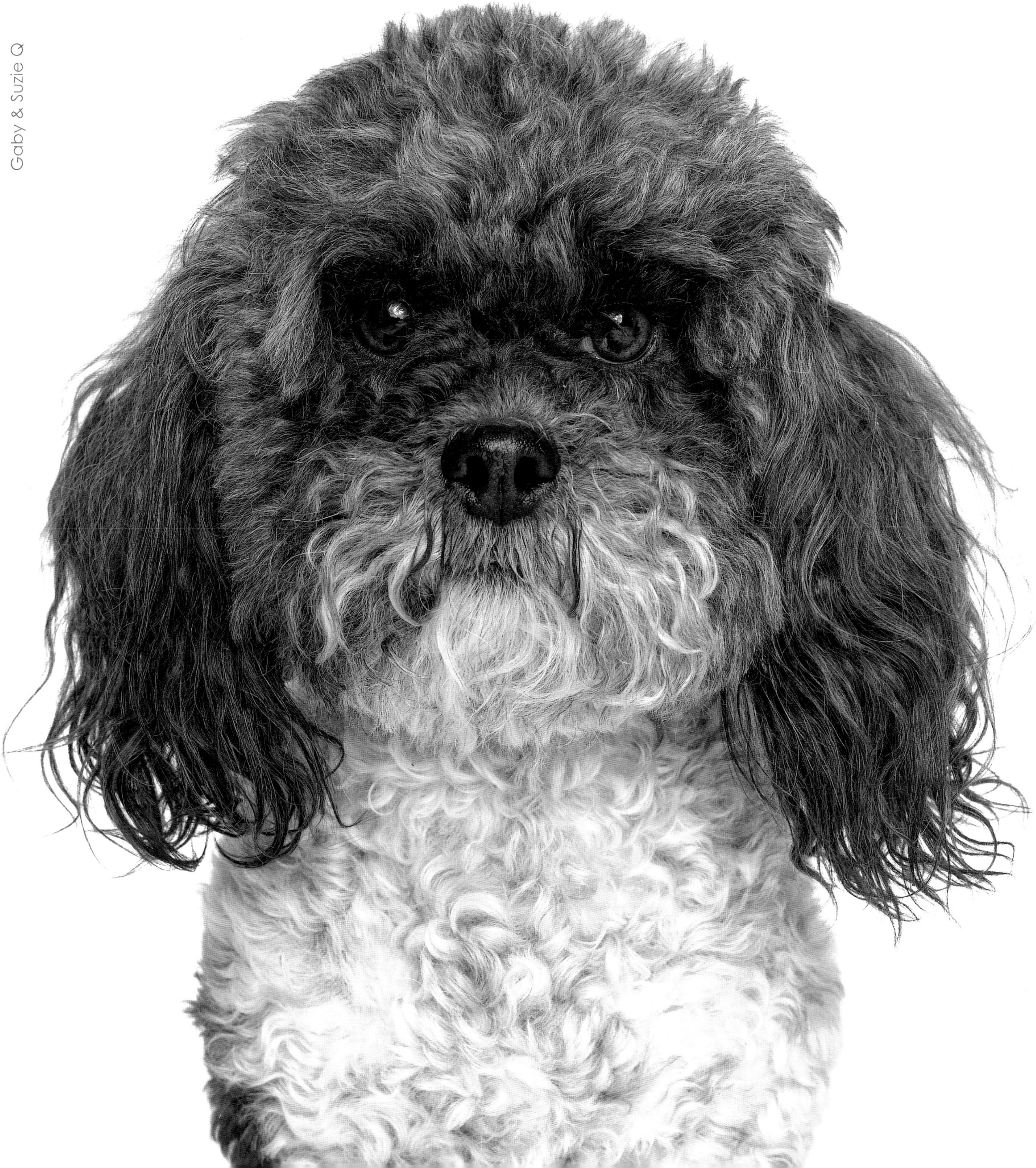

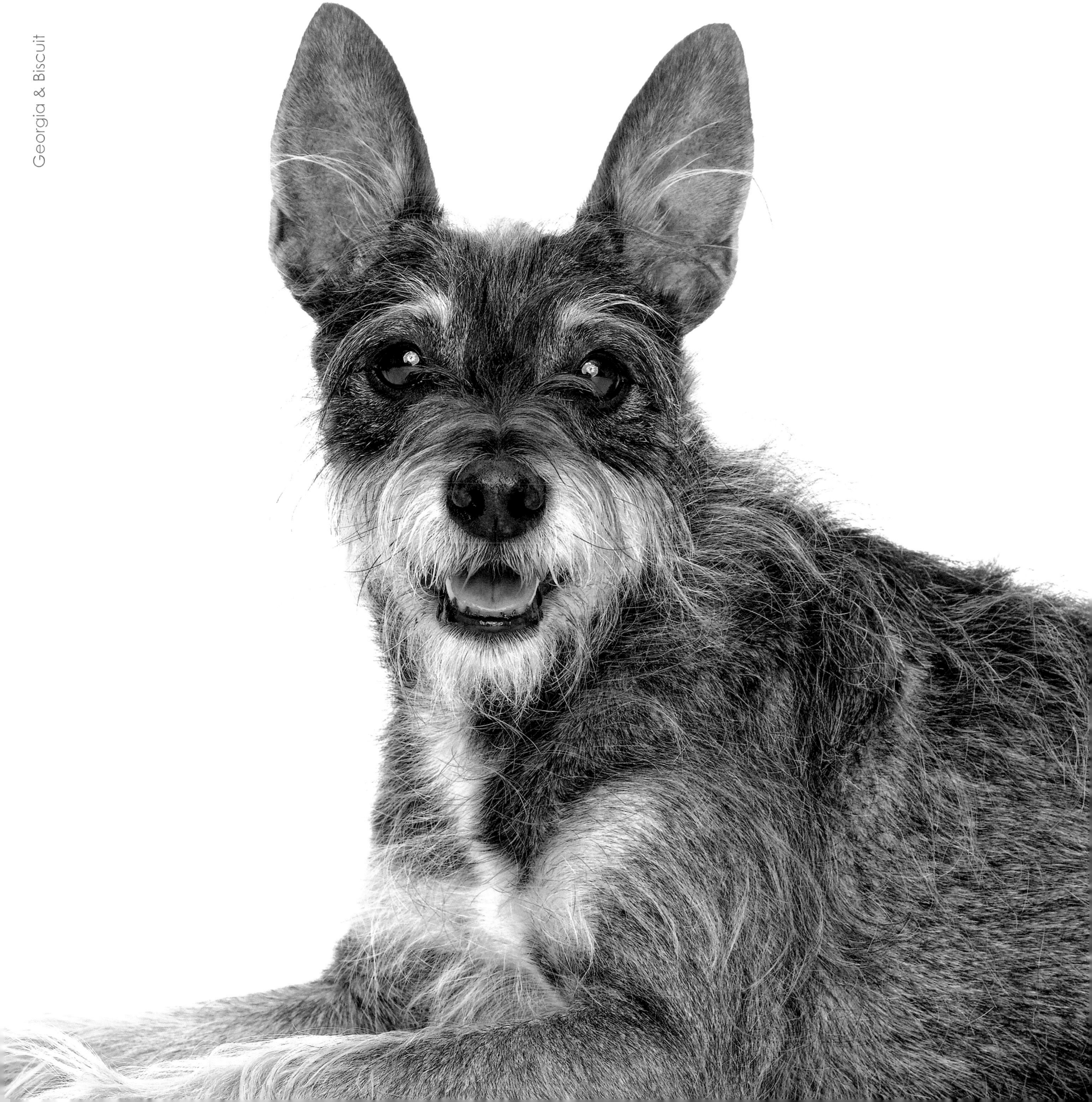

Riglee & Jedi

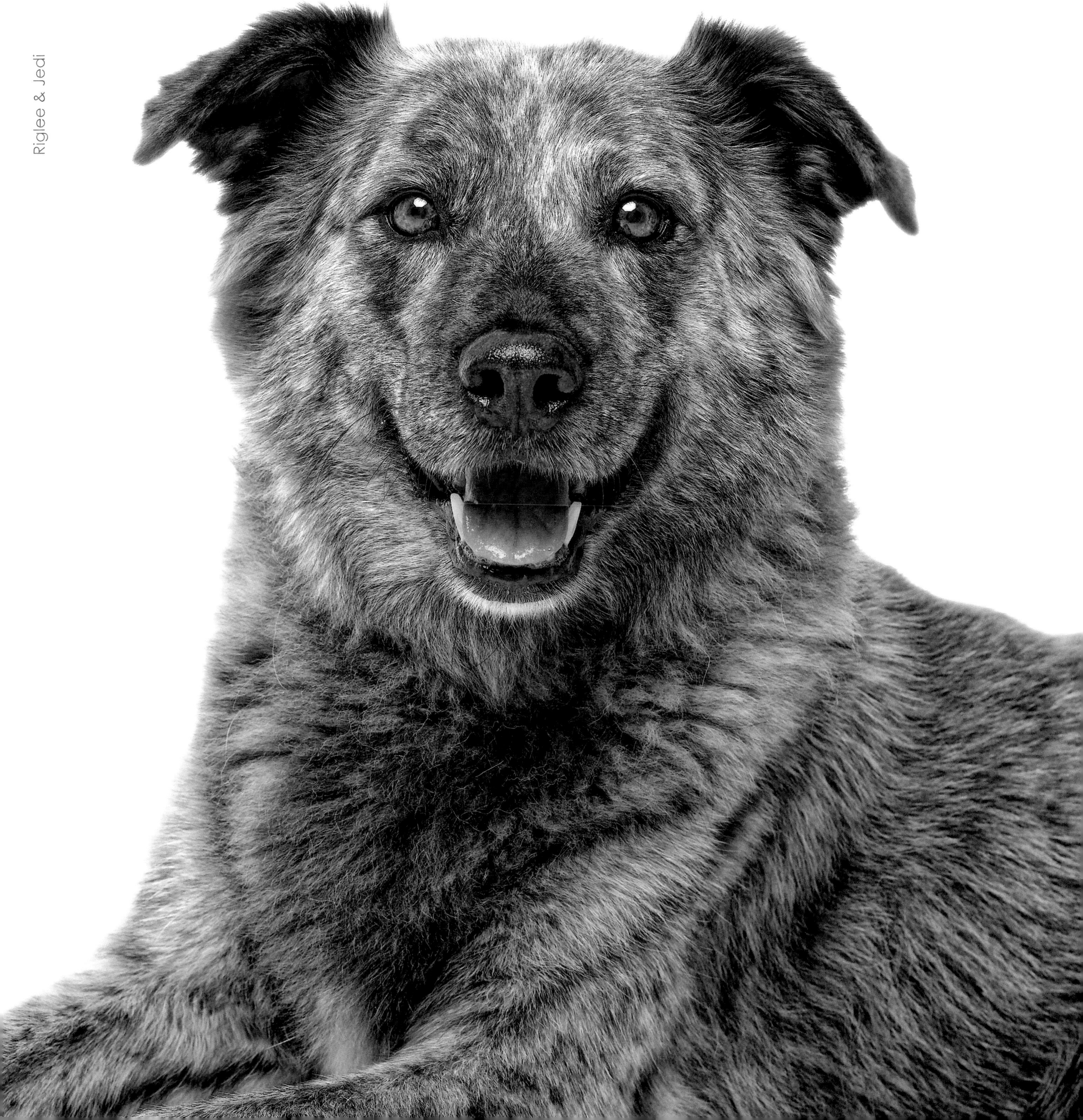

Hendrix & Reggie

Kota

Skye & Blue

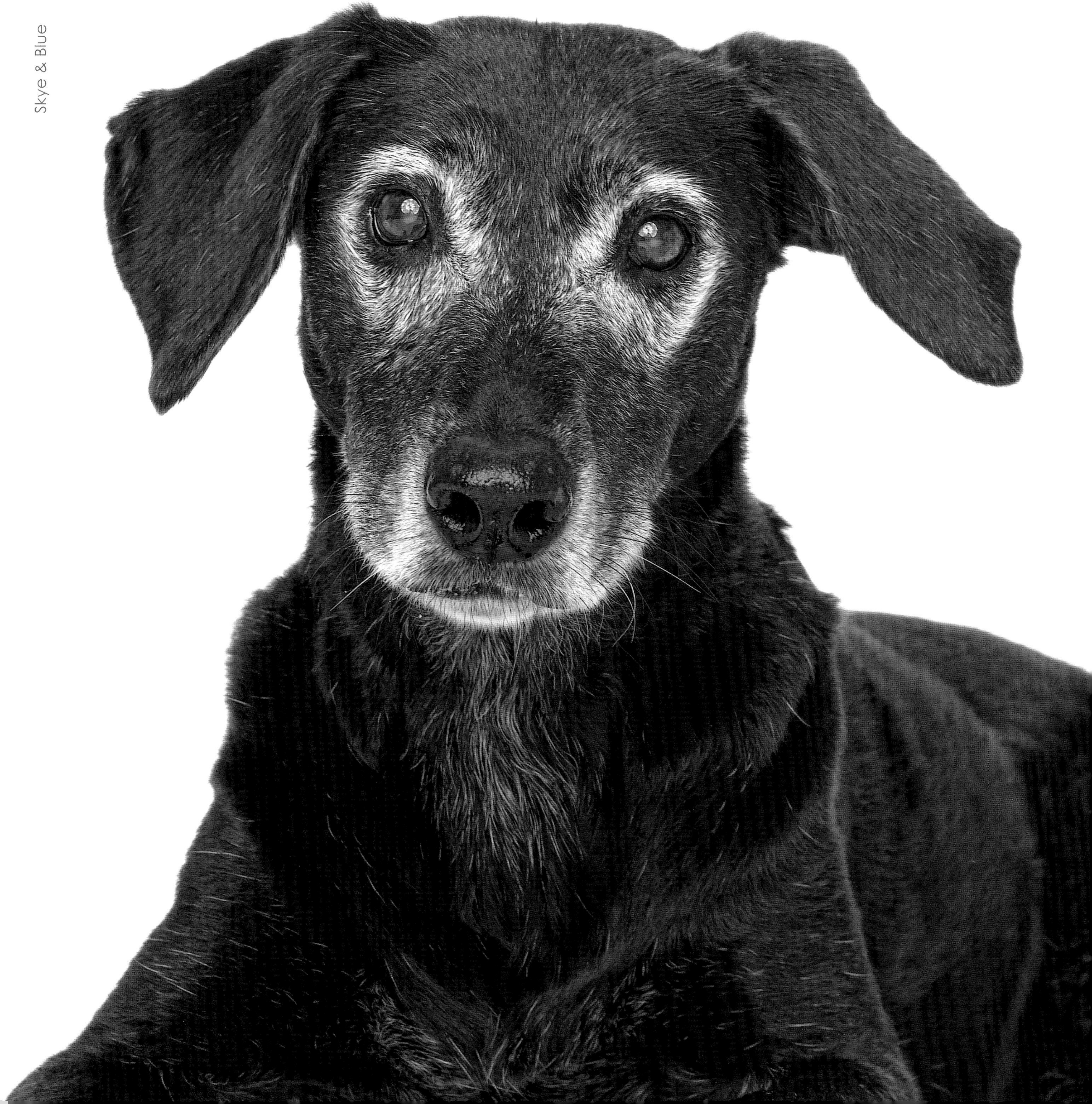

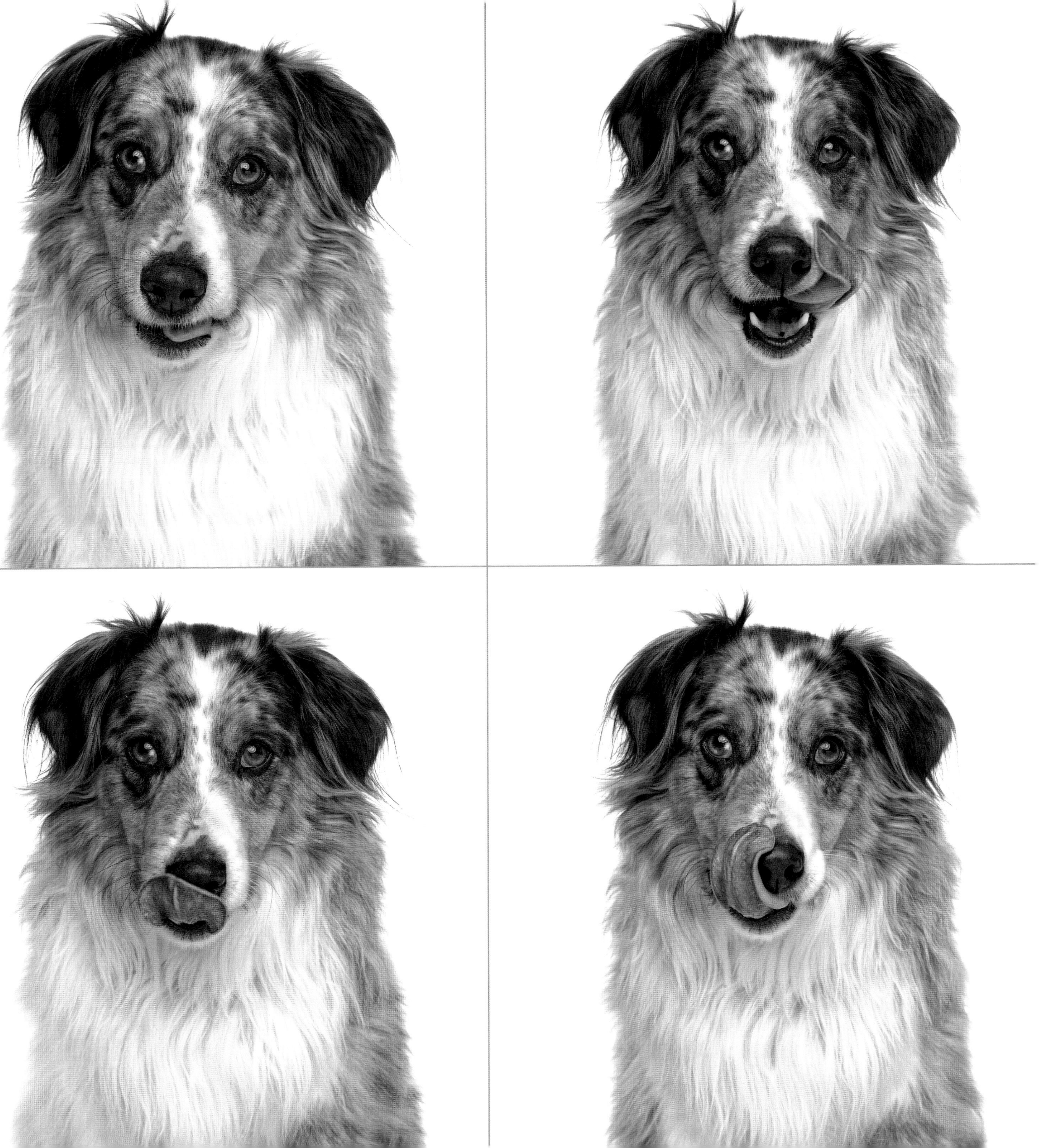

Kyra & Maxwell

Chance & Sydney

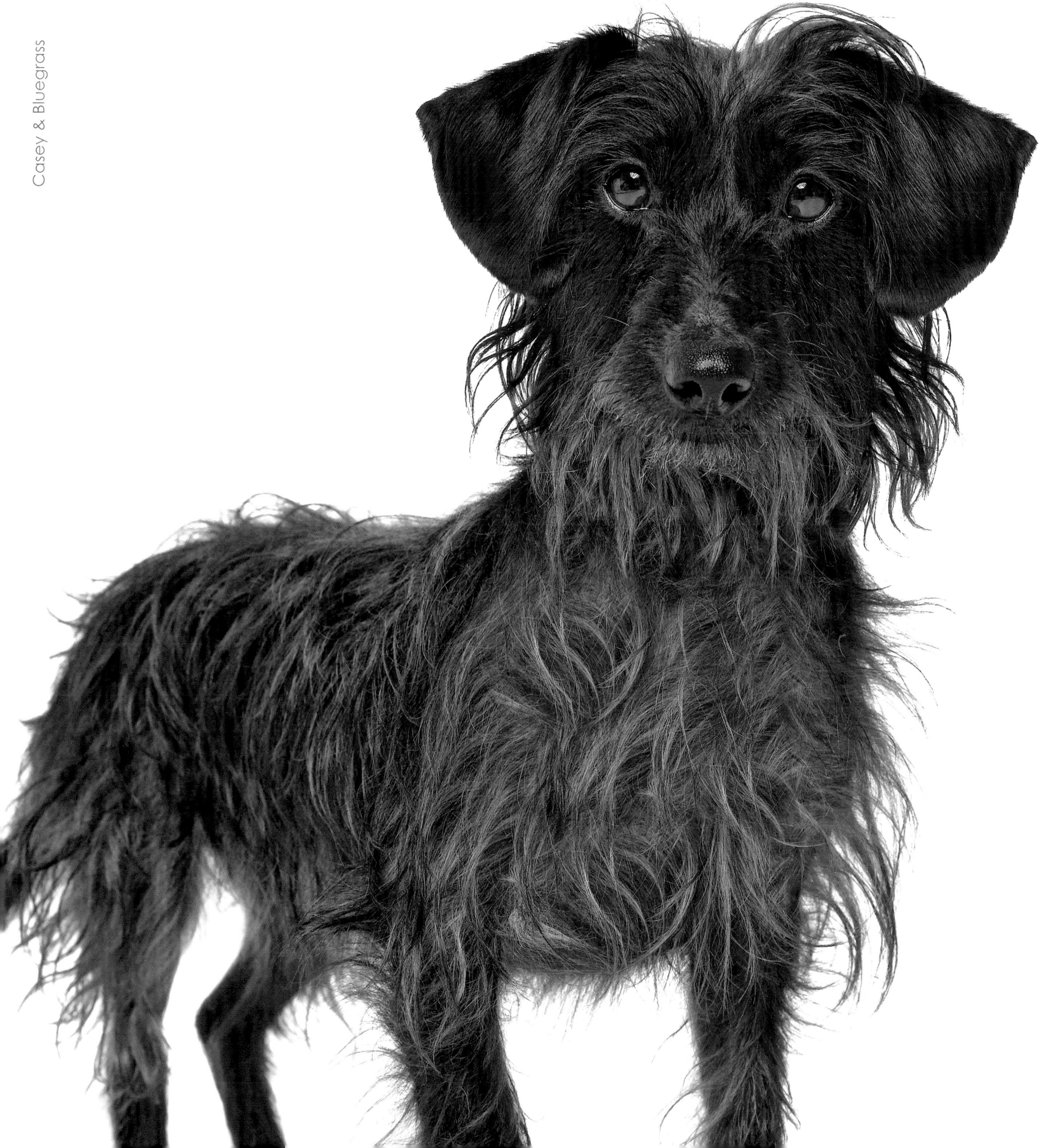

Casey & Bluegrass

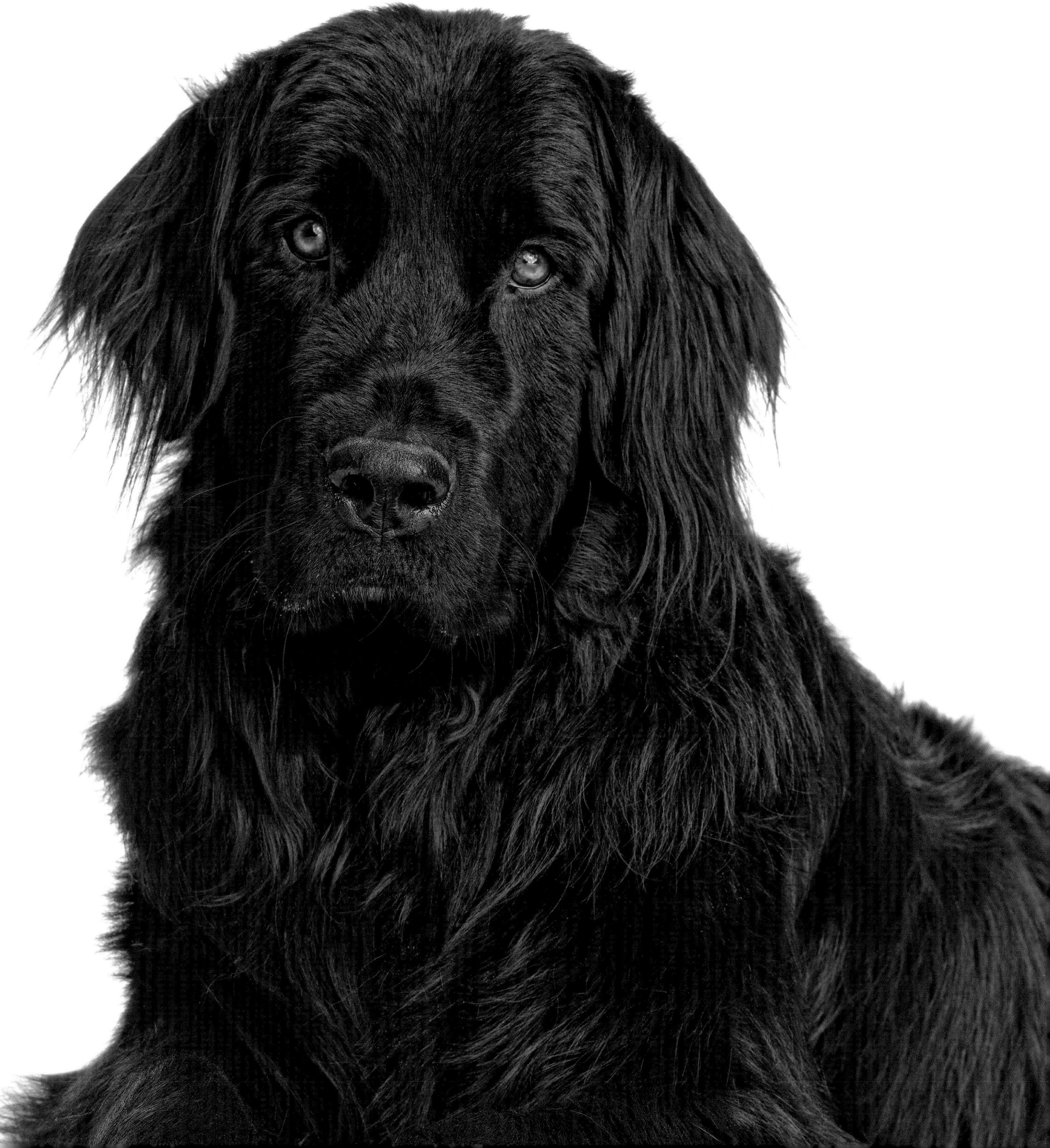

Lou & Marley

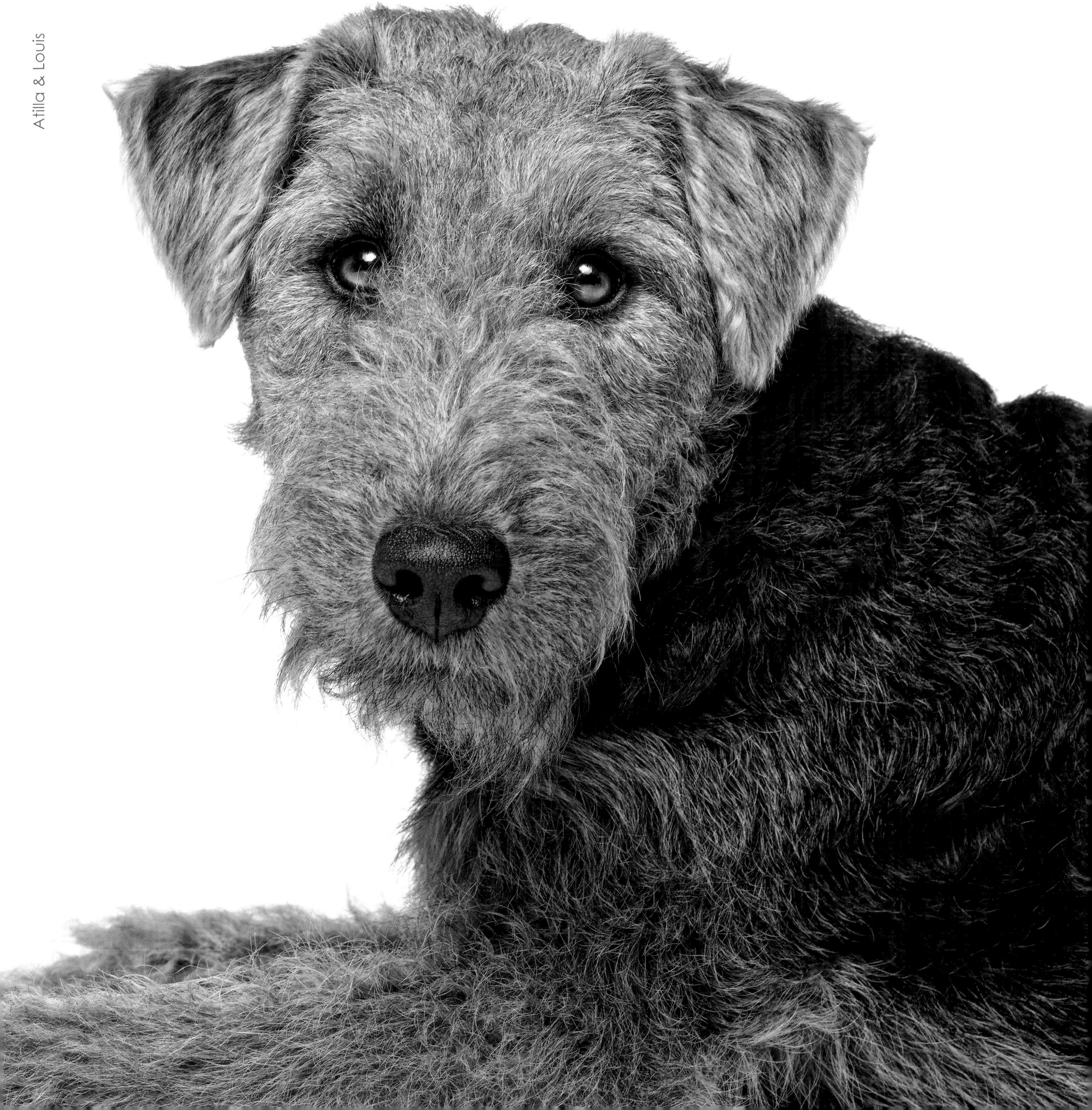

Atilla & Louis

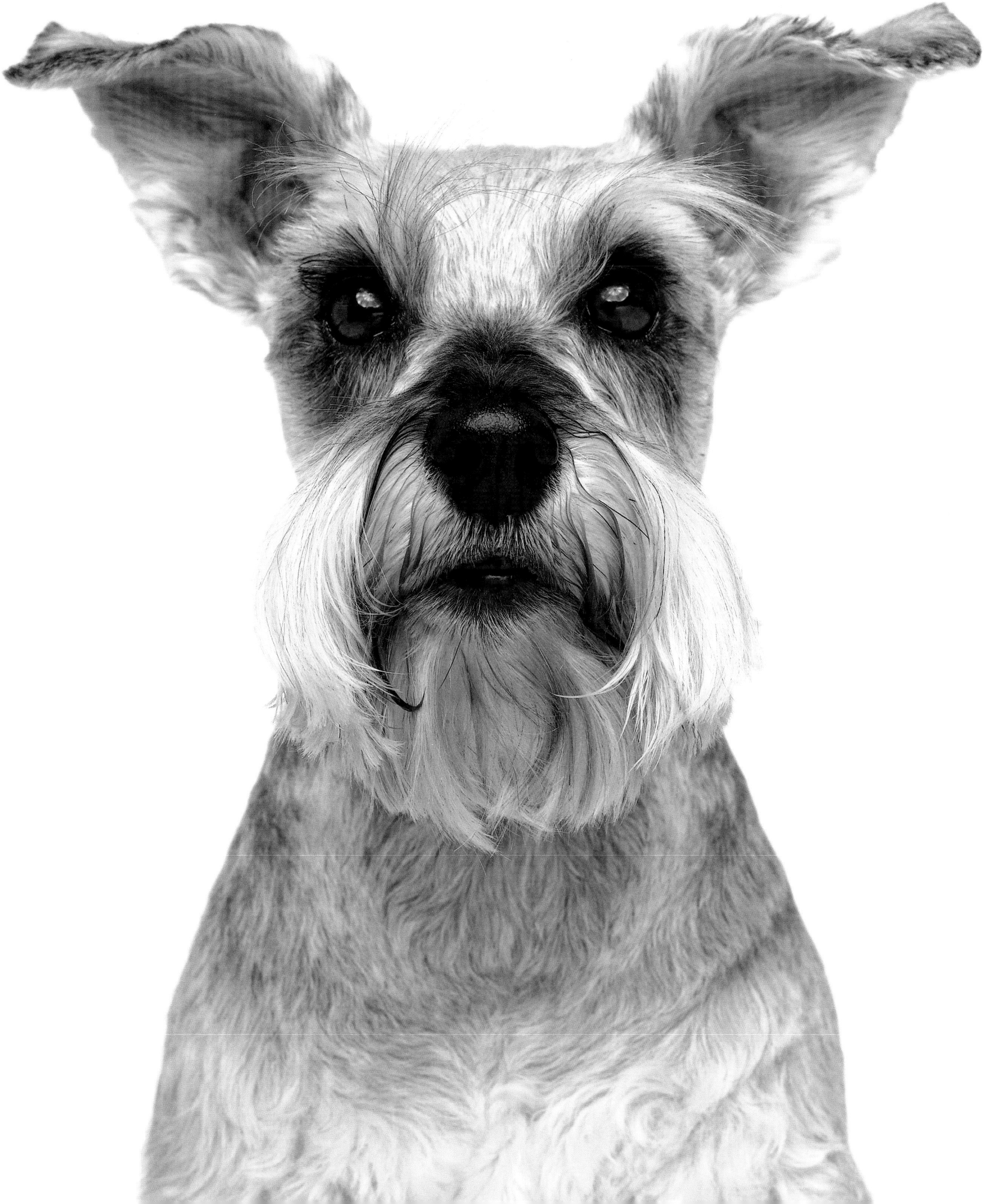

Maddie & Pandora

Ivy & Rigby

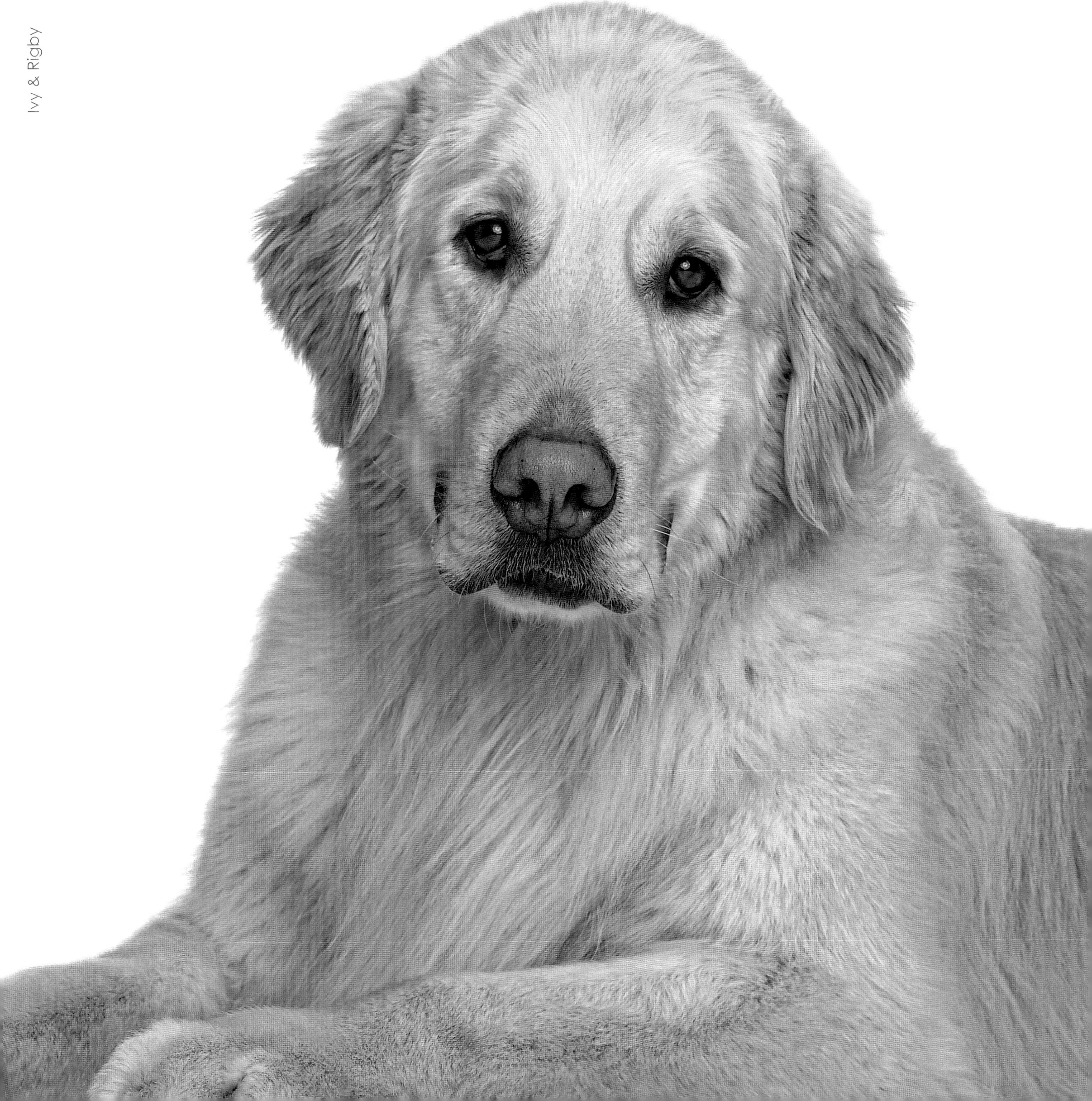

Kuma

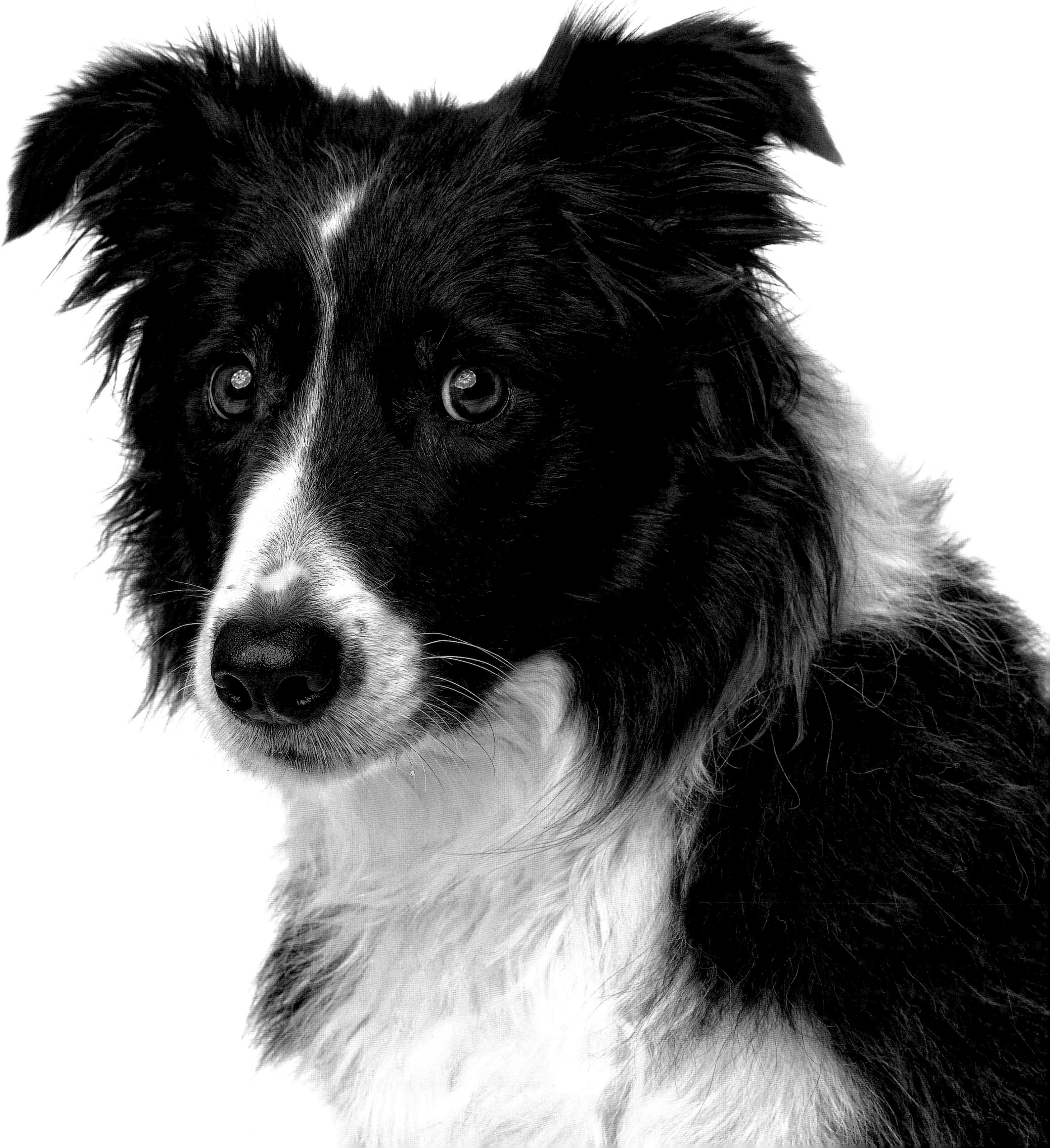

Meeko & Skid

Lucy & Bouncy

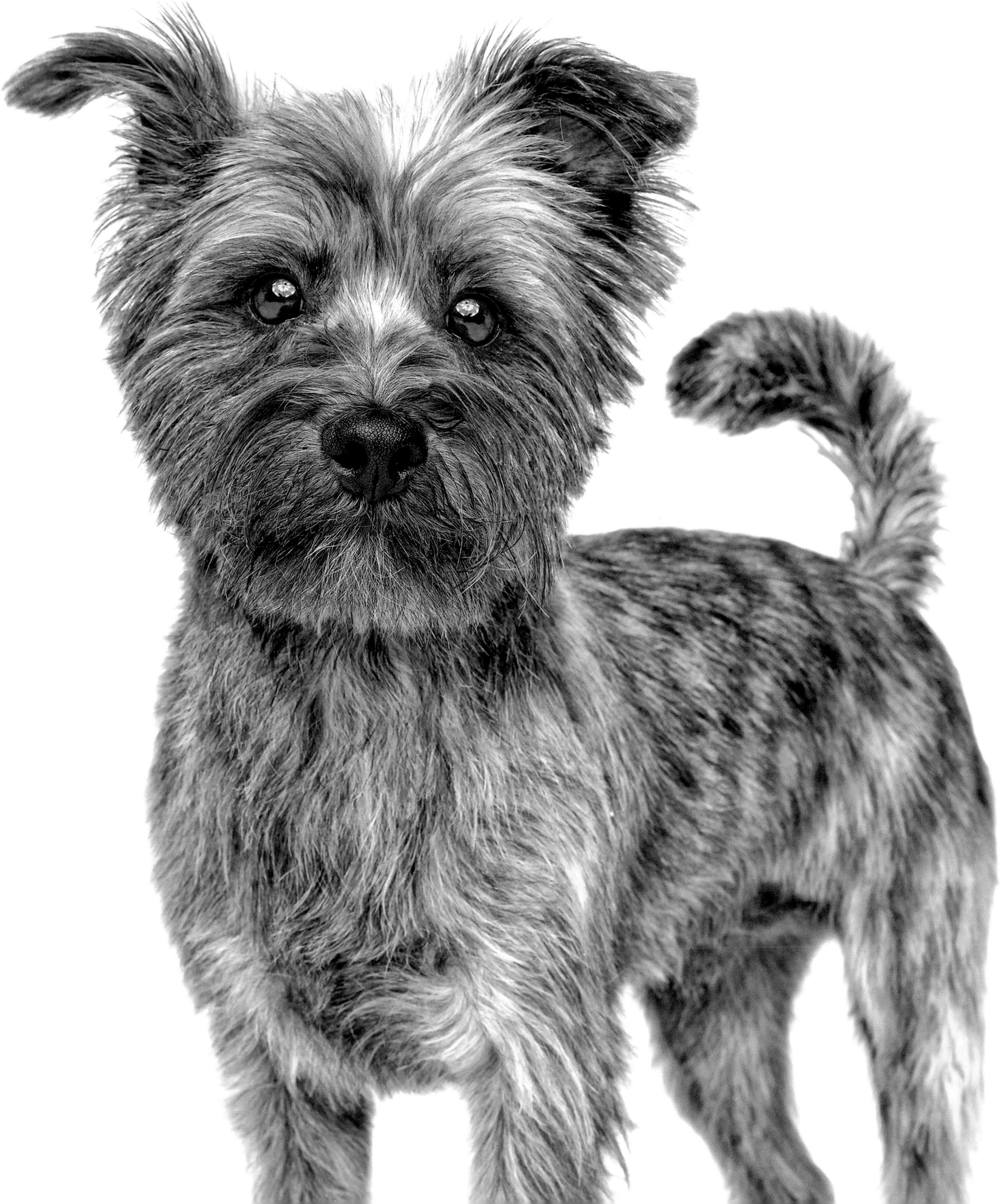

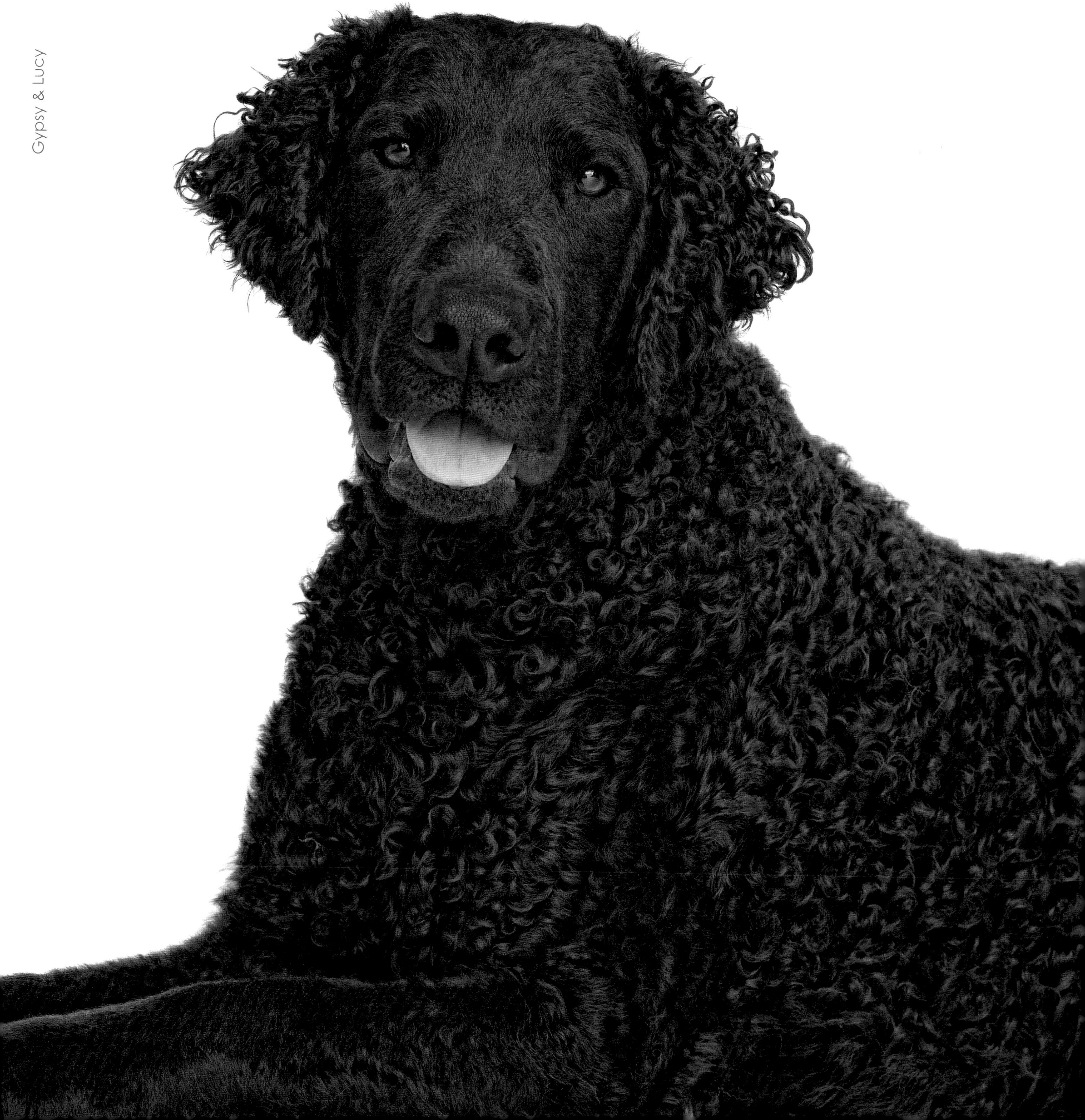

Gypsy & Lucy

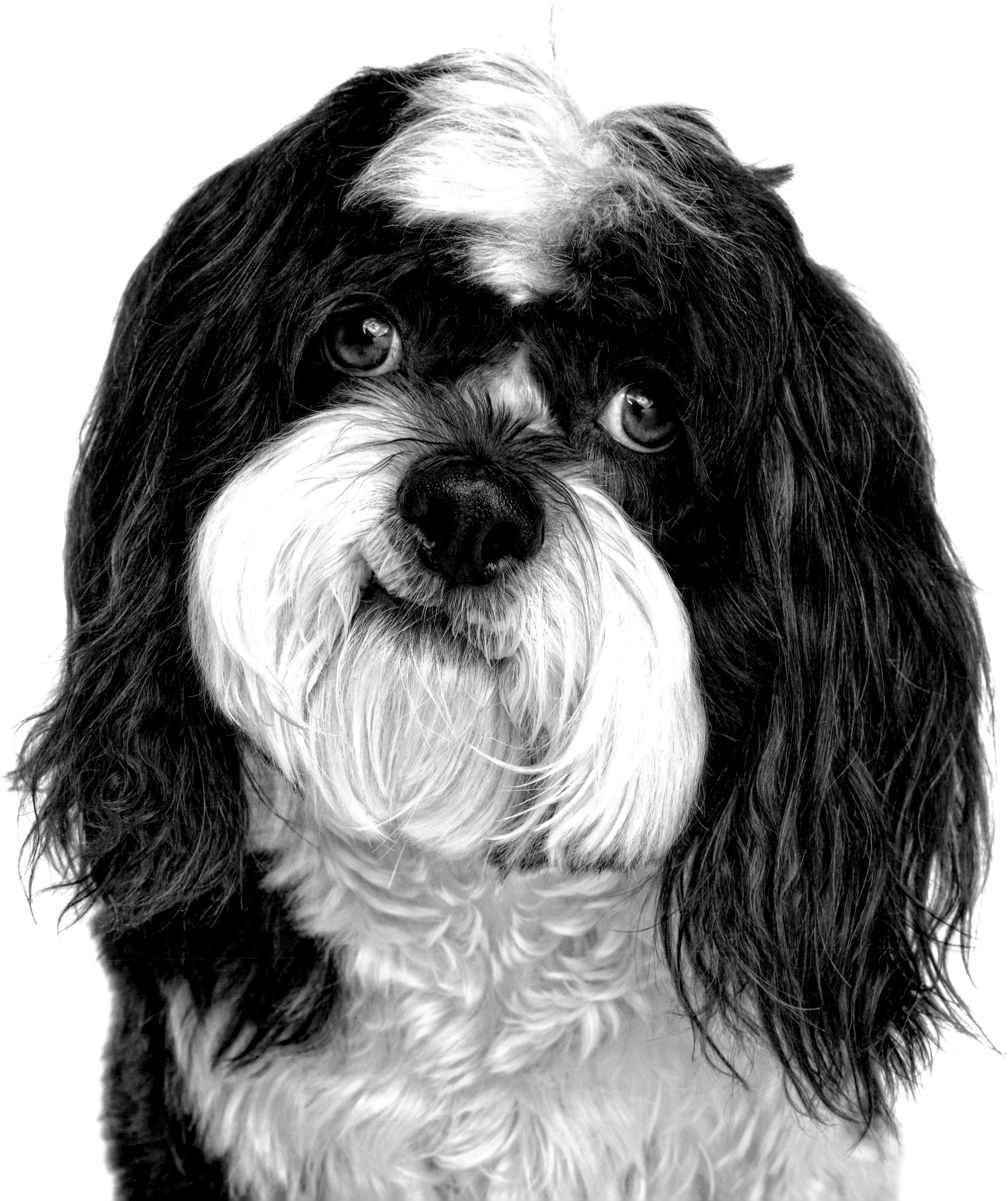

Herbie & Nacho

Maxwell & Lola

Billie Holiday & Fenway

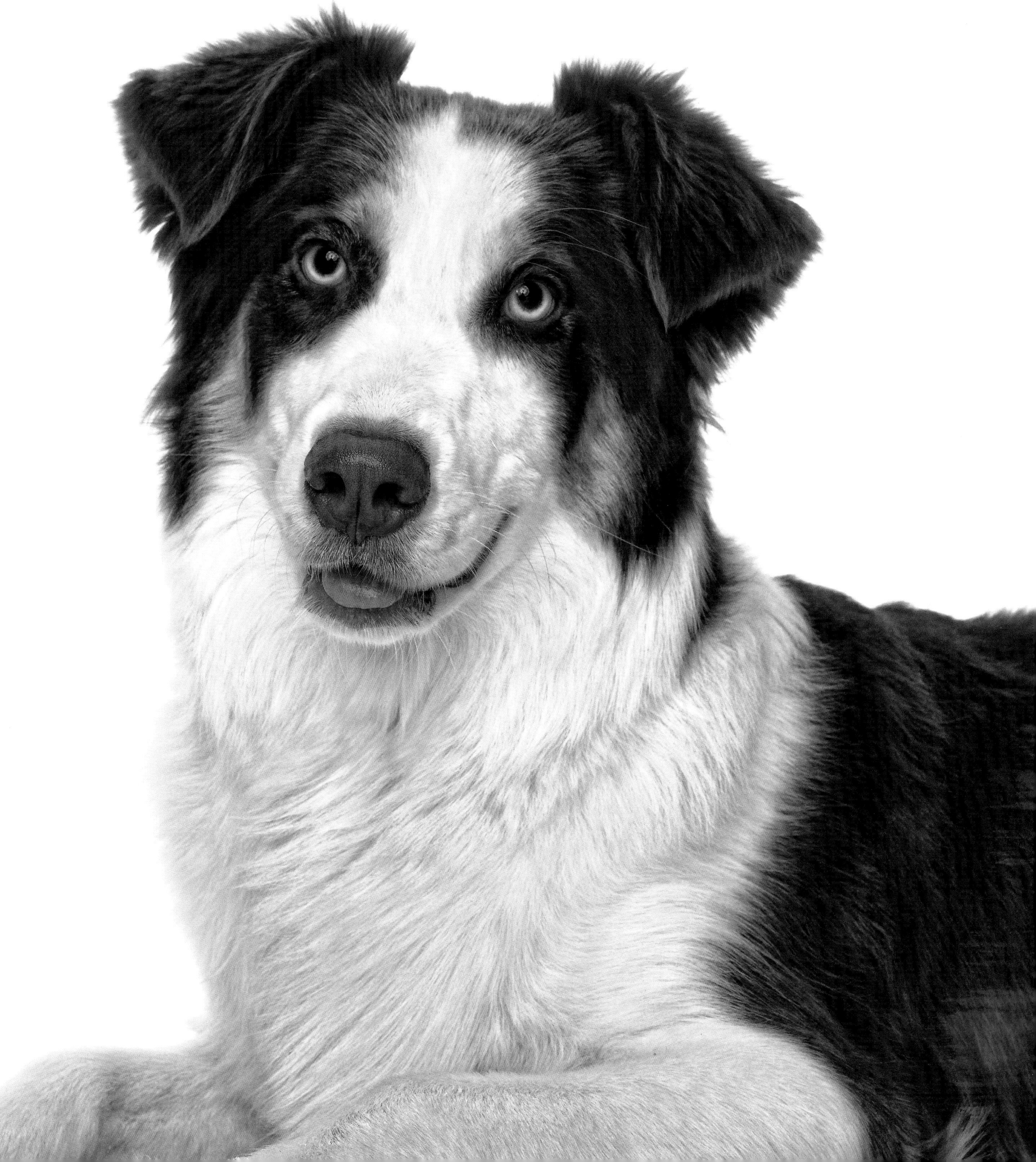

Sammy & Kirby

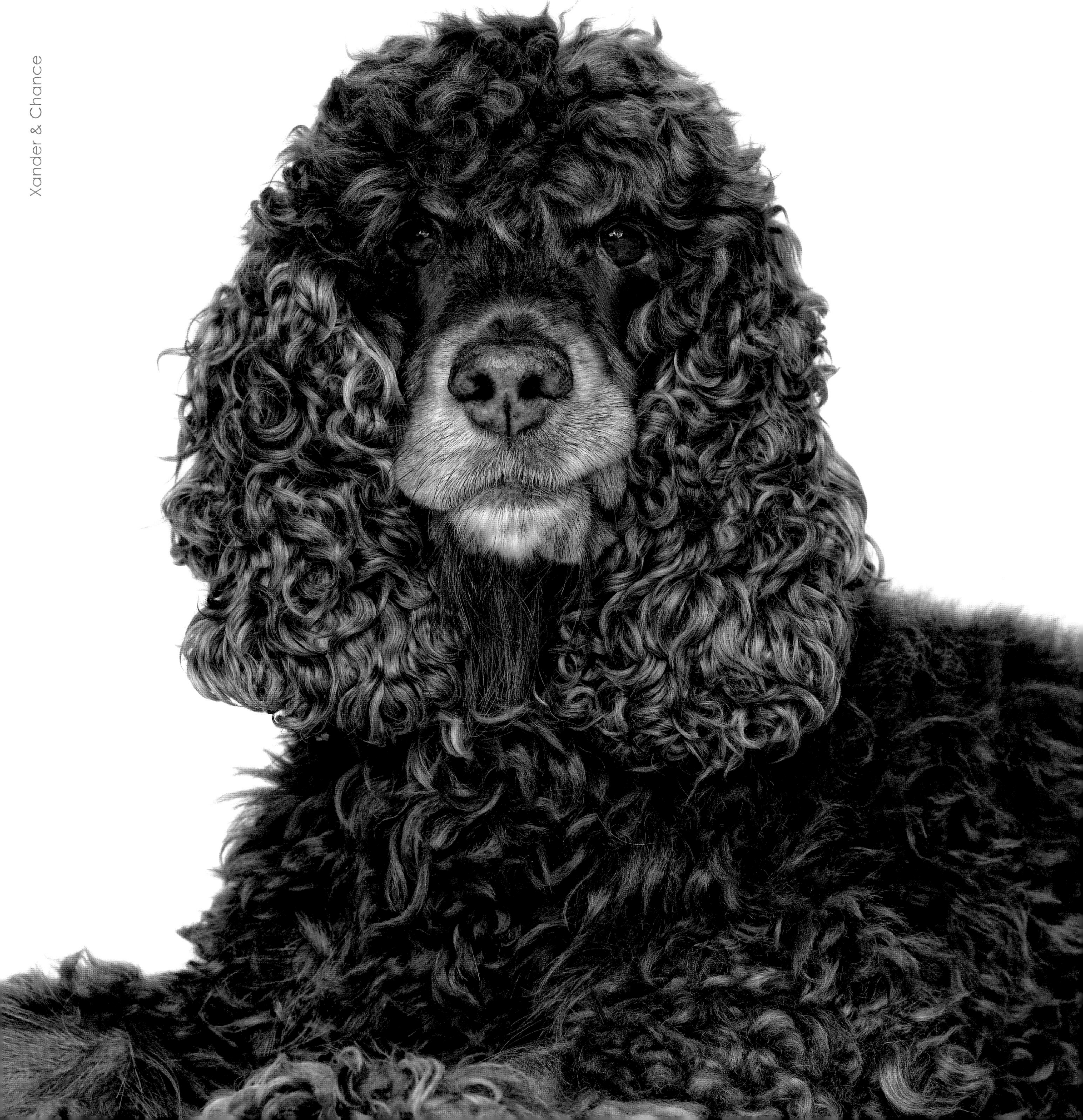

Xander & Chance

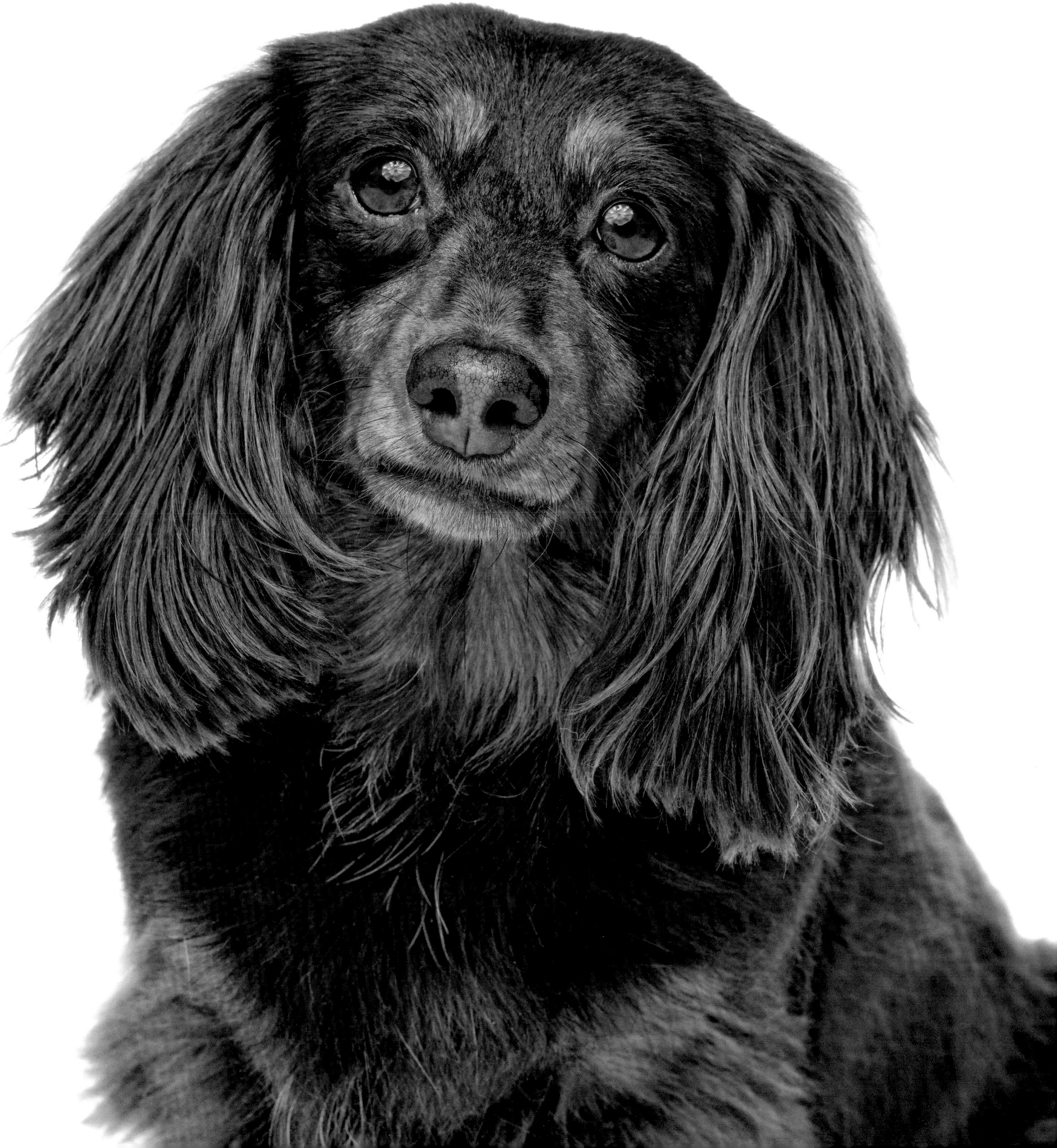

JAGS & Moxie

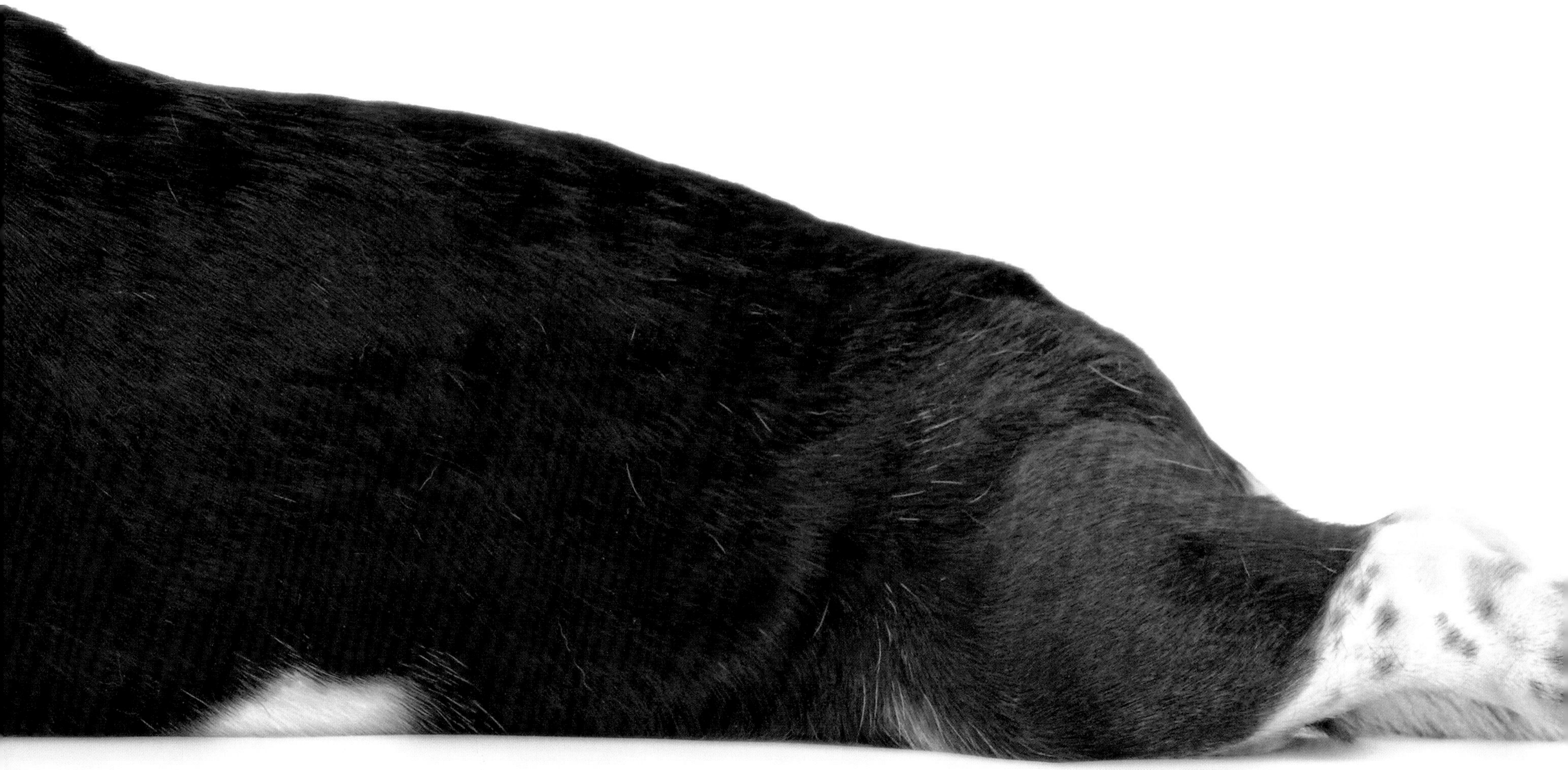

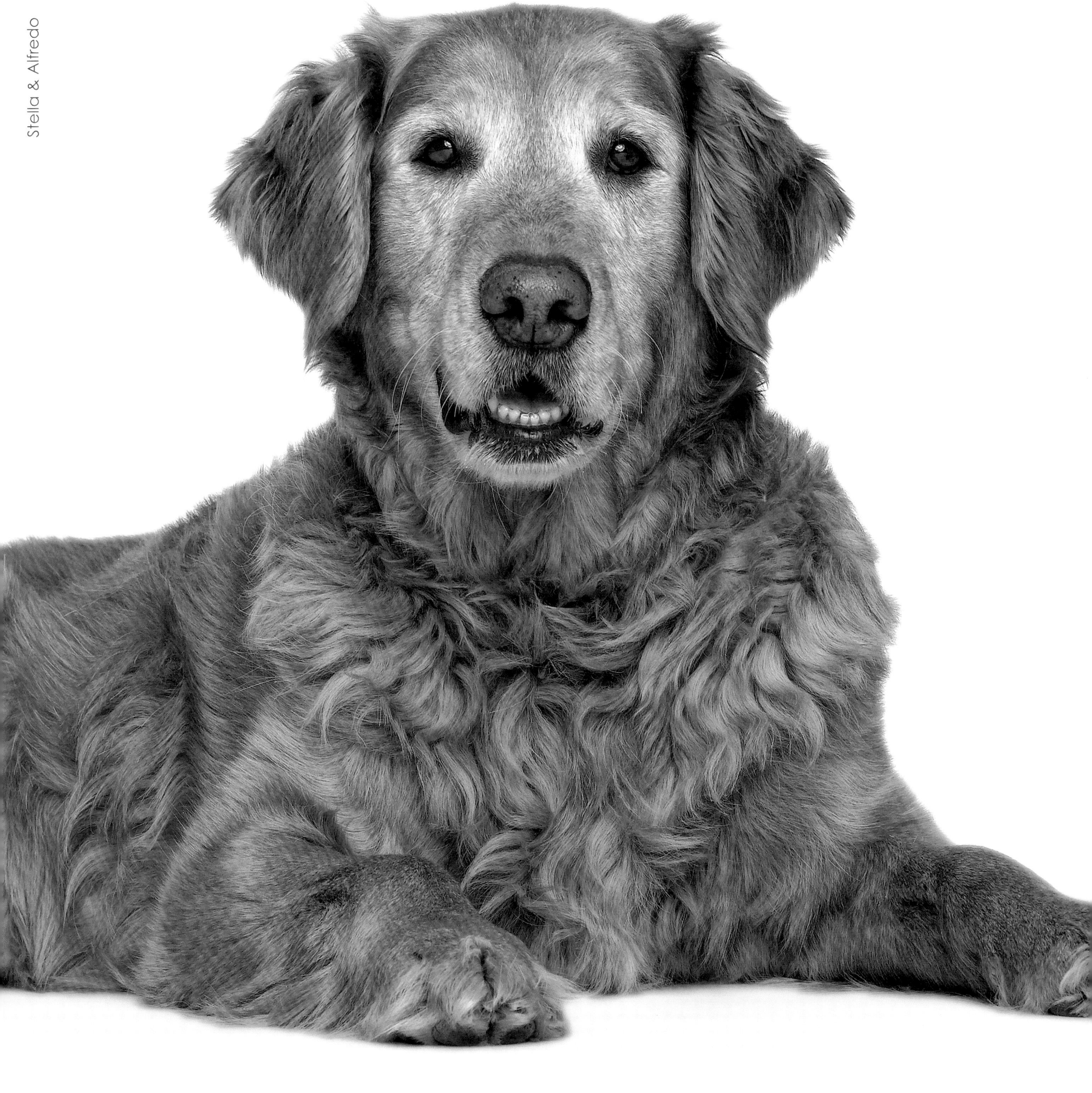

Stella & Alfredo

Betty & Dixie

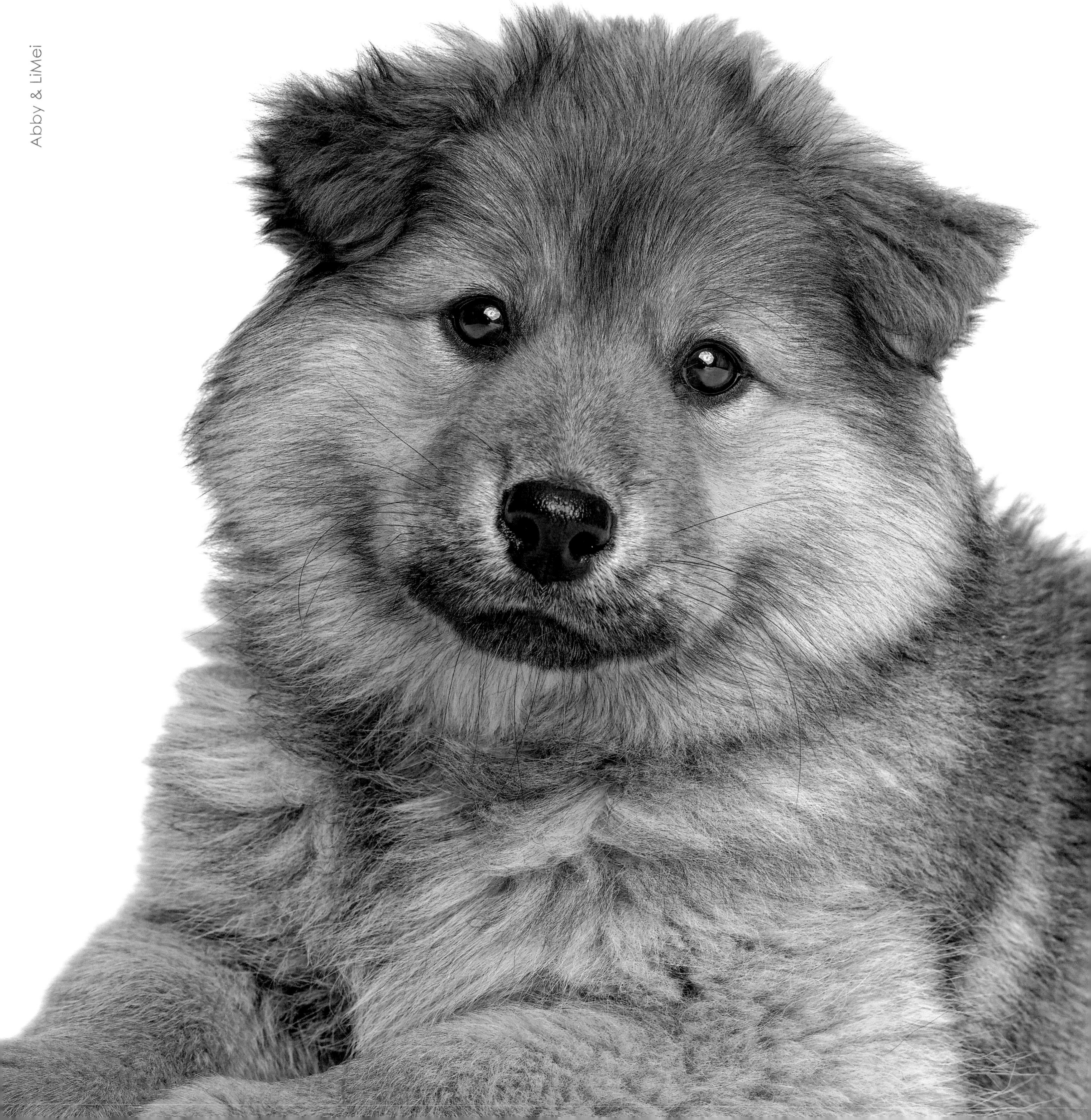

Abby & LiMei

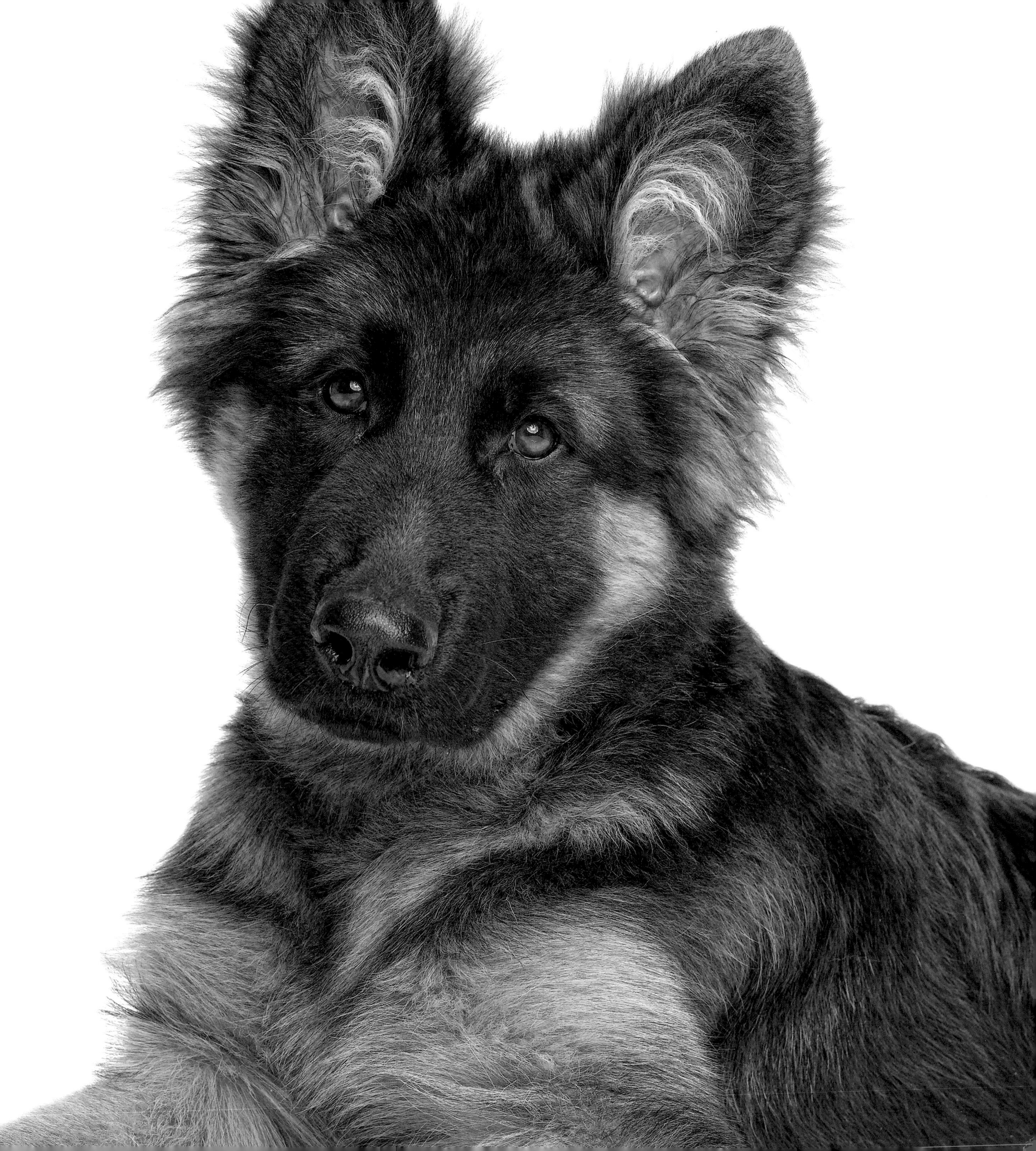

Hank & Max

Roscoe & Sima

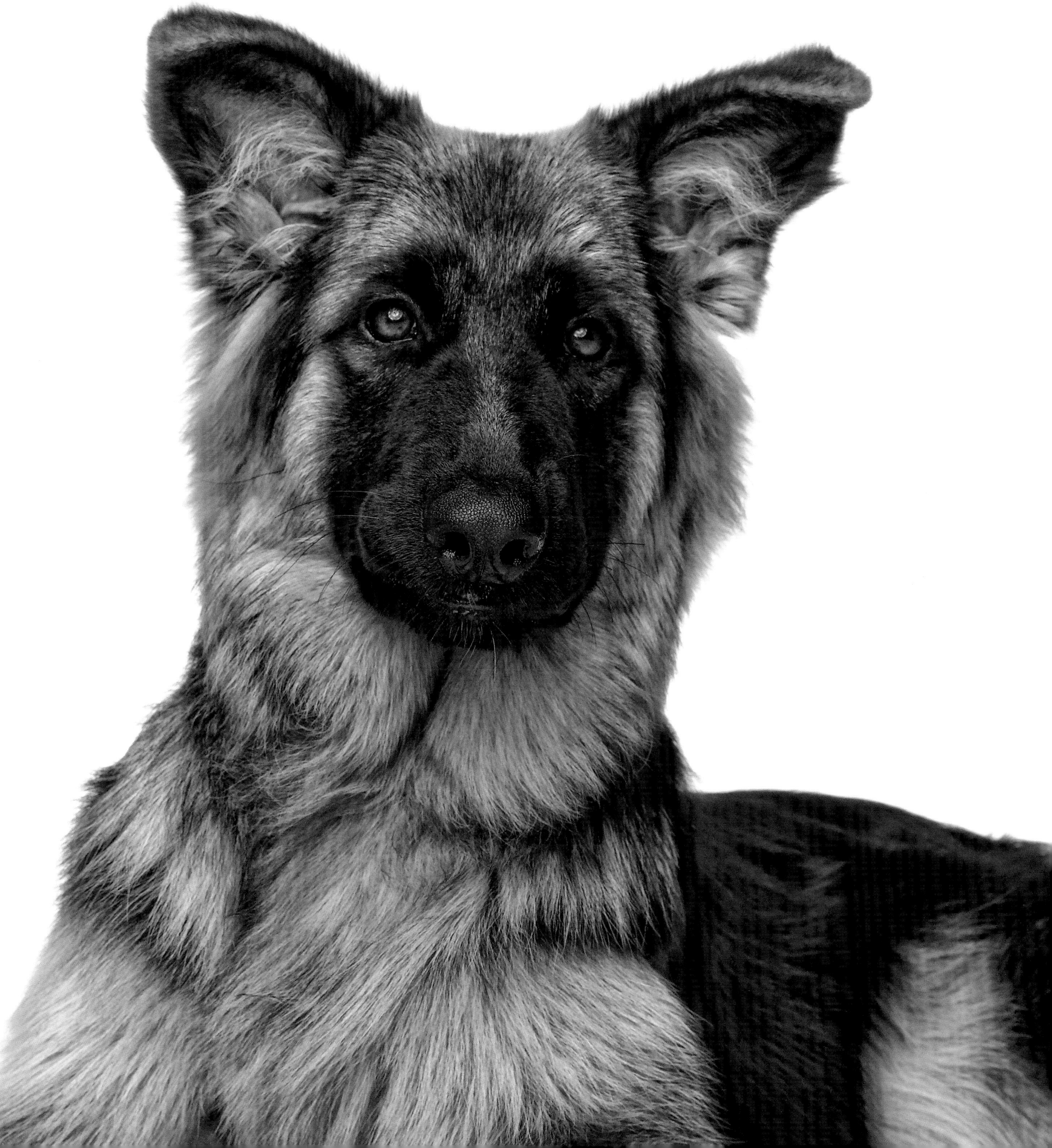

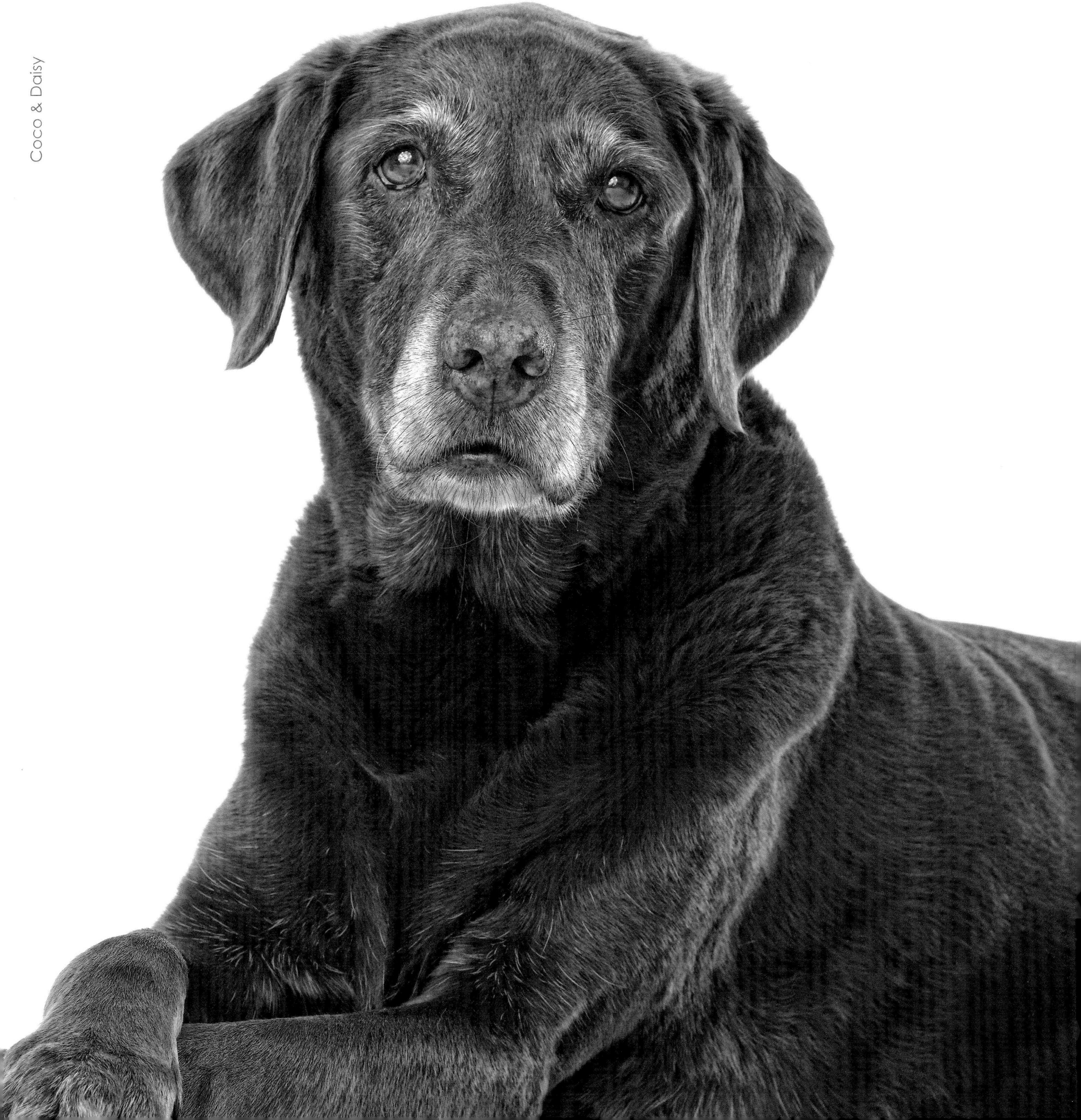

Coco & Daisy

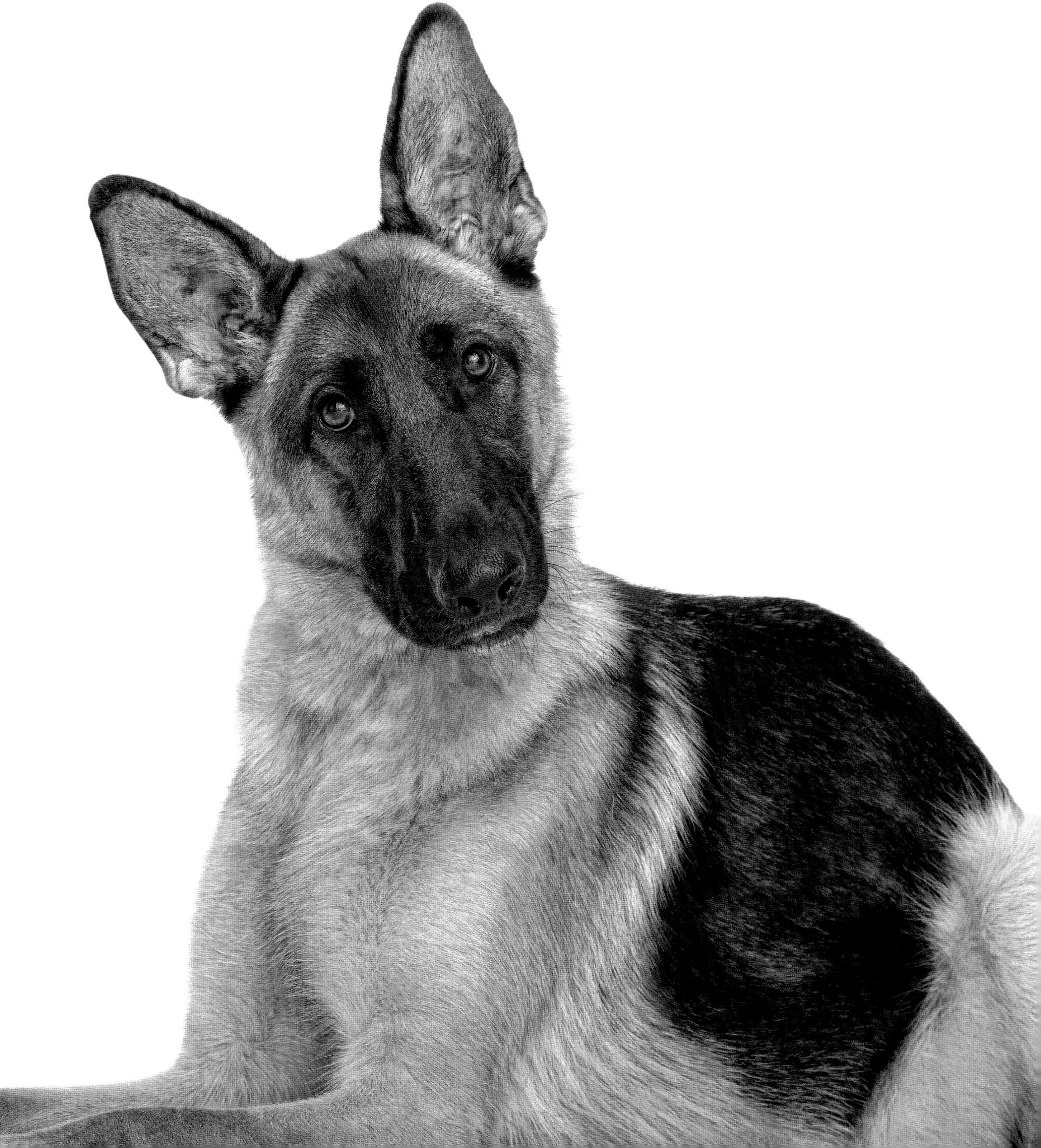

Homeless in 2013 & Pualani

Asta

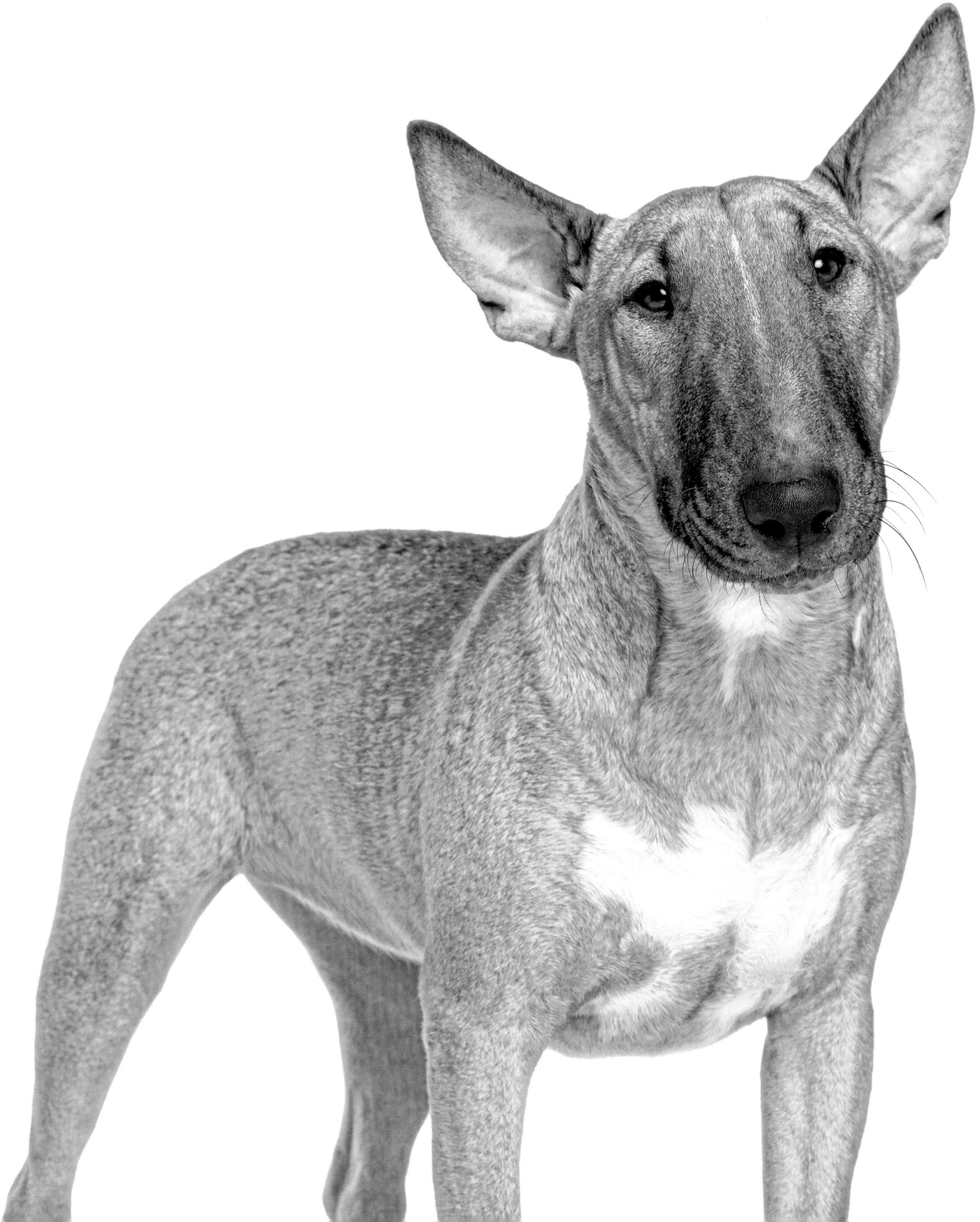
Charlie & Zoe

Pinot & Mookie

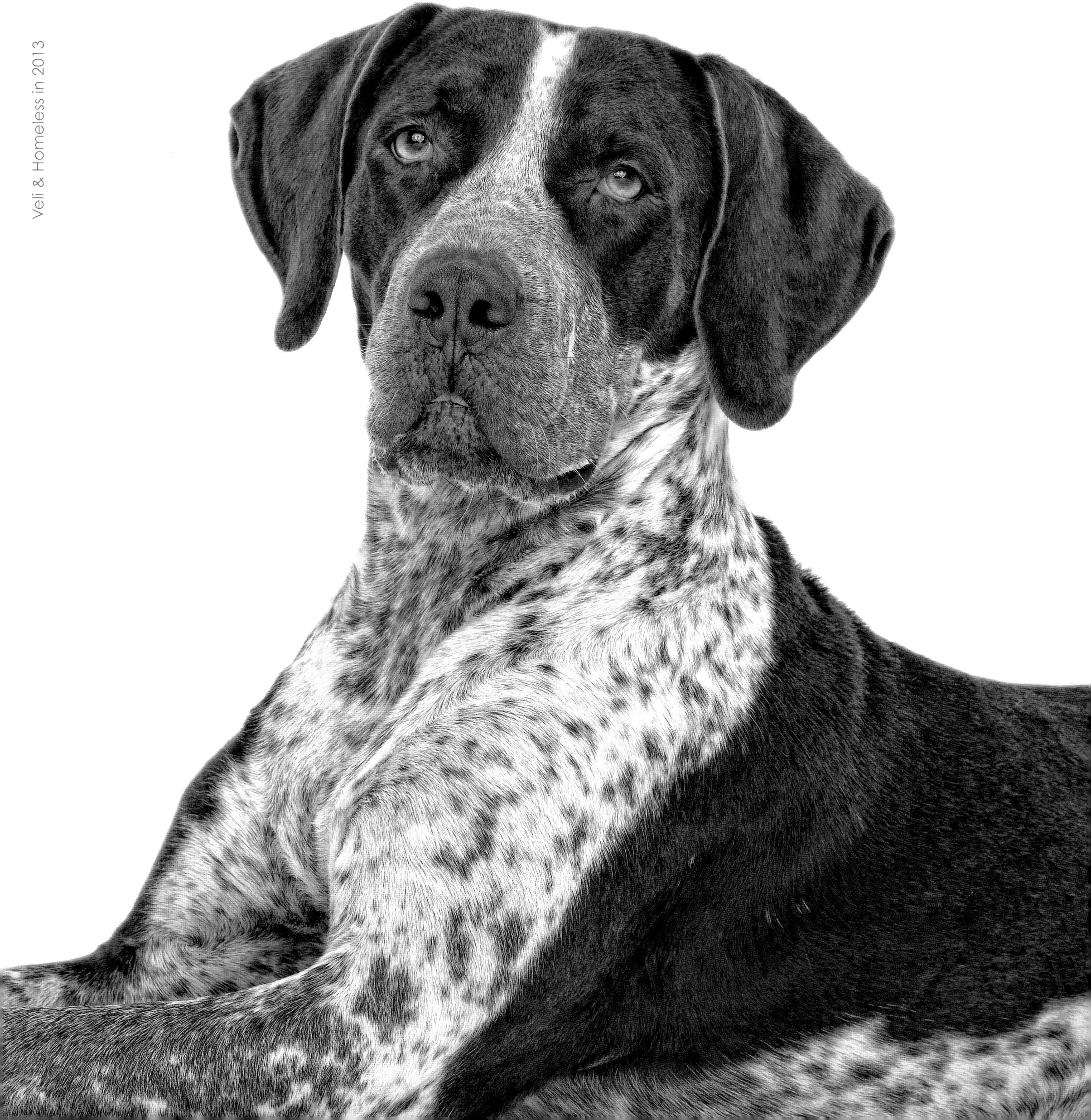

Veli & Homeless in 2013

Hugo & Gulliver

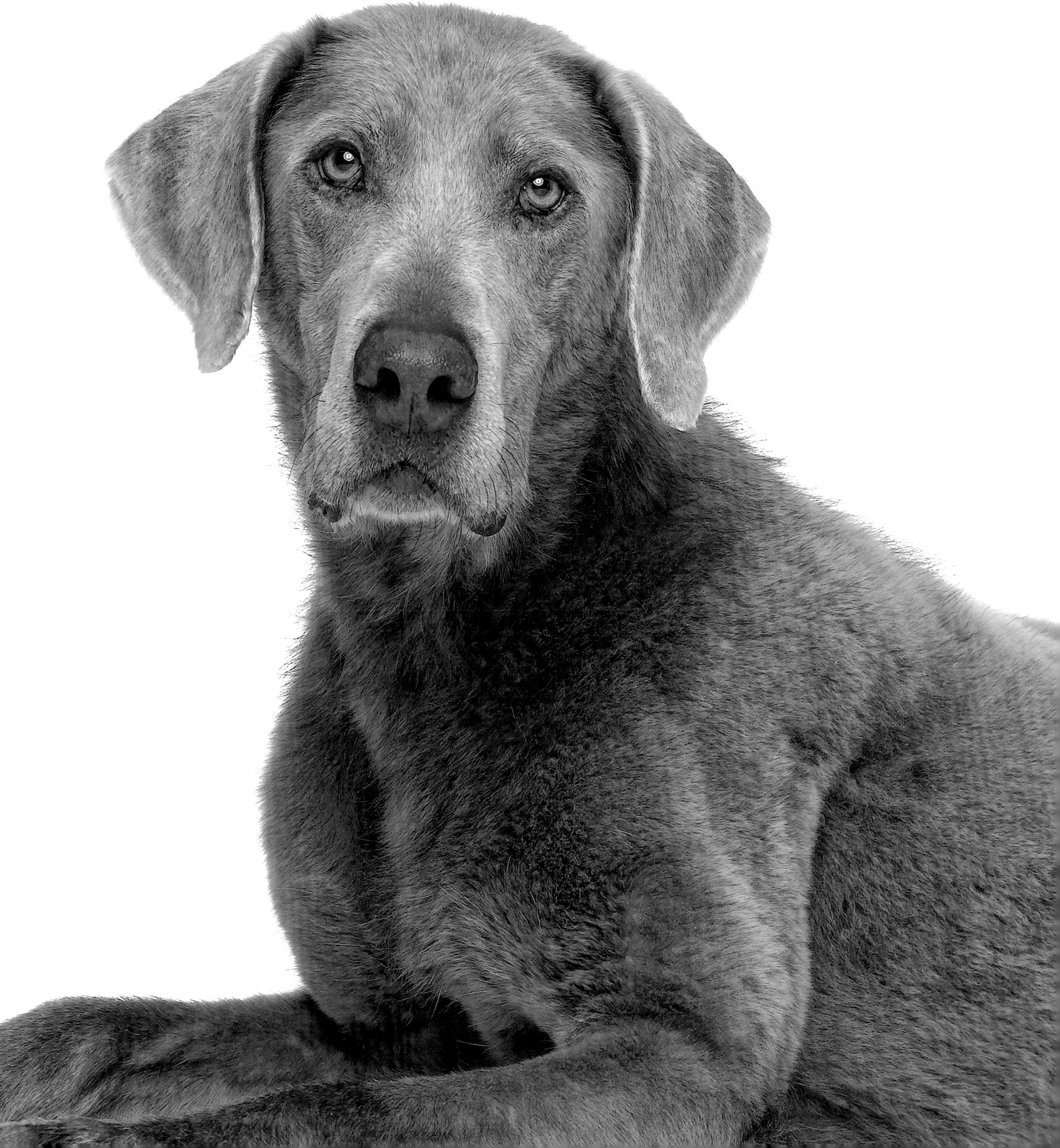

Montana & Victor

Jack & Cassie

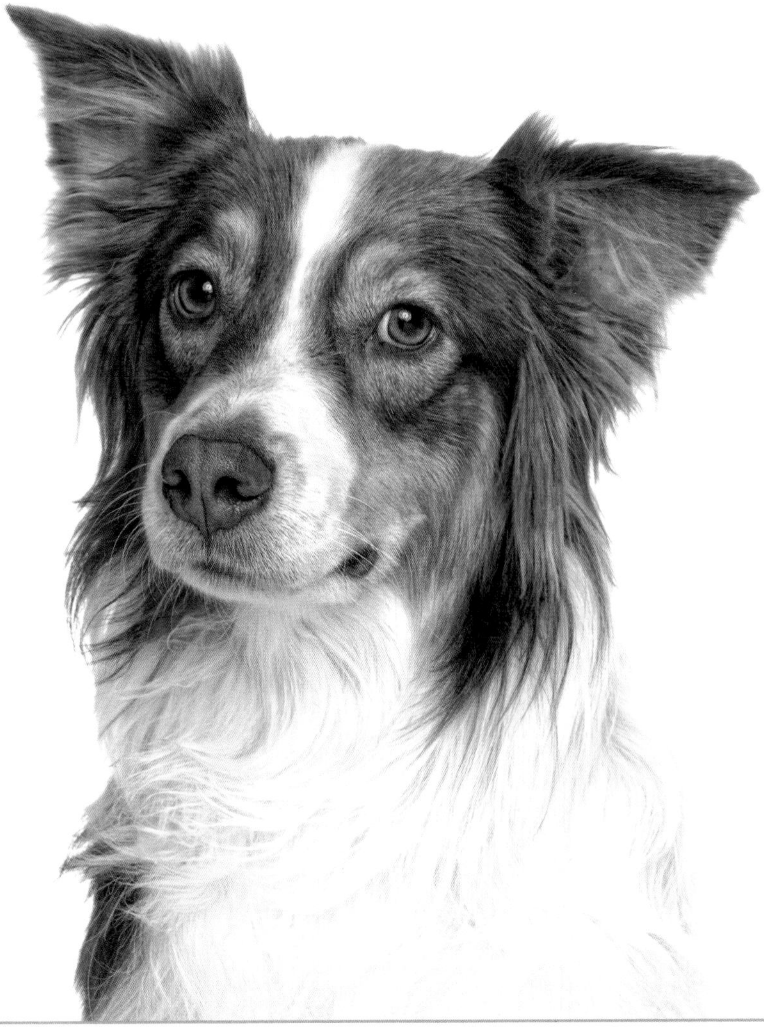
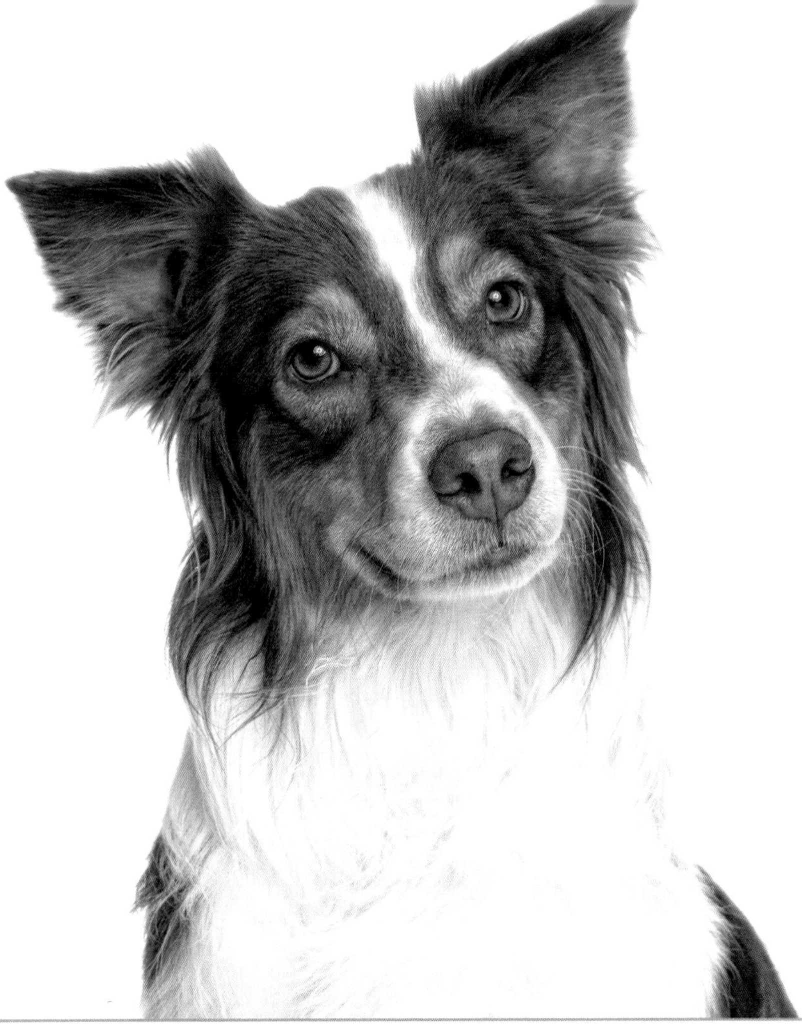
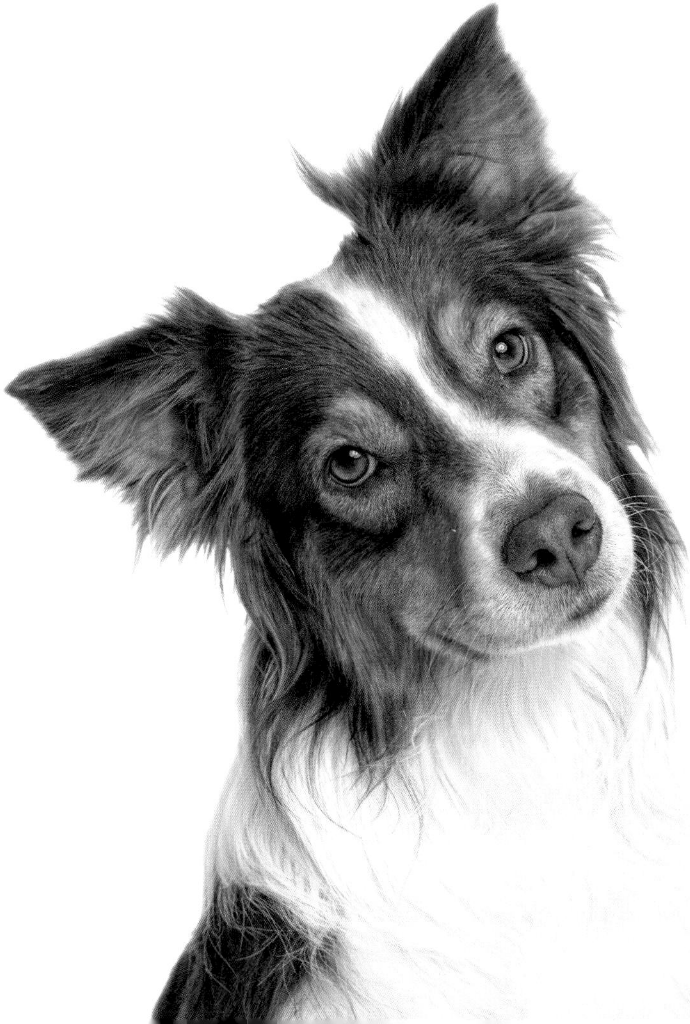
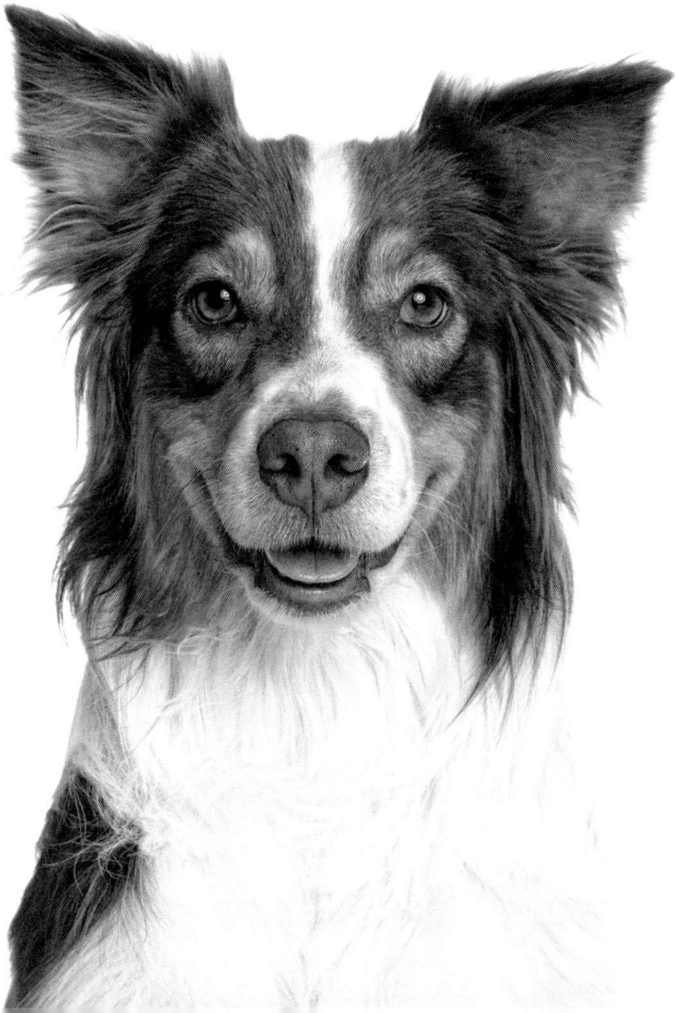

Fozzie Bear & Annie

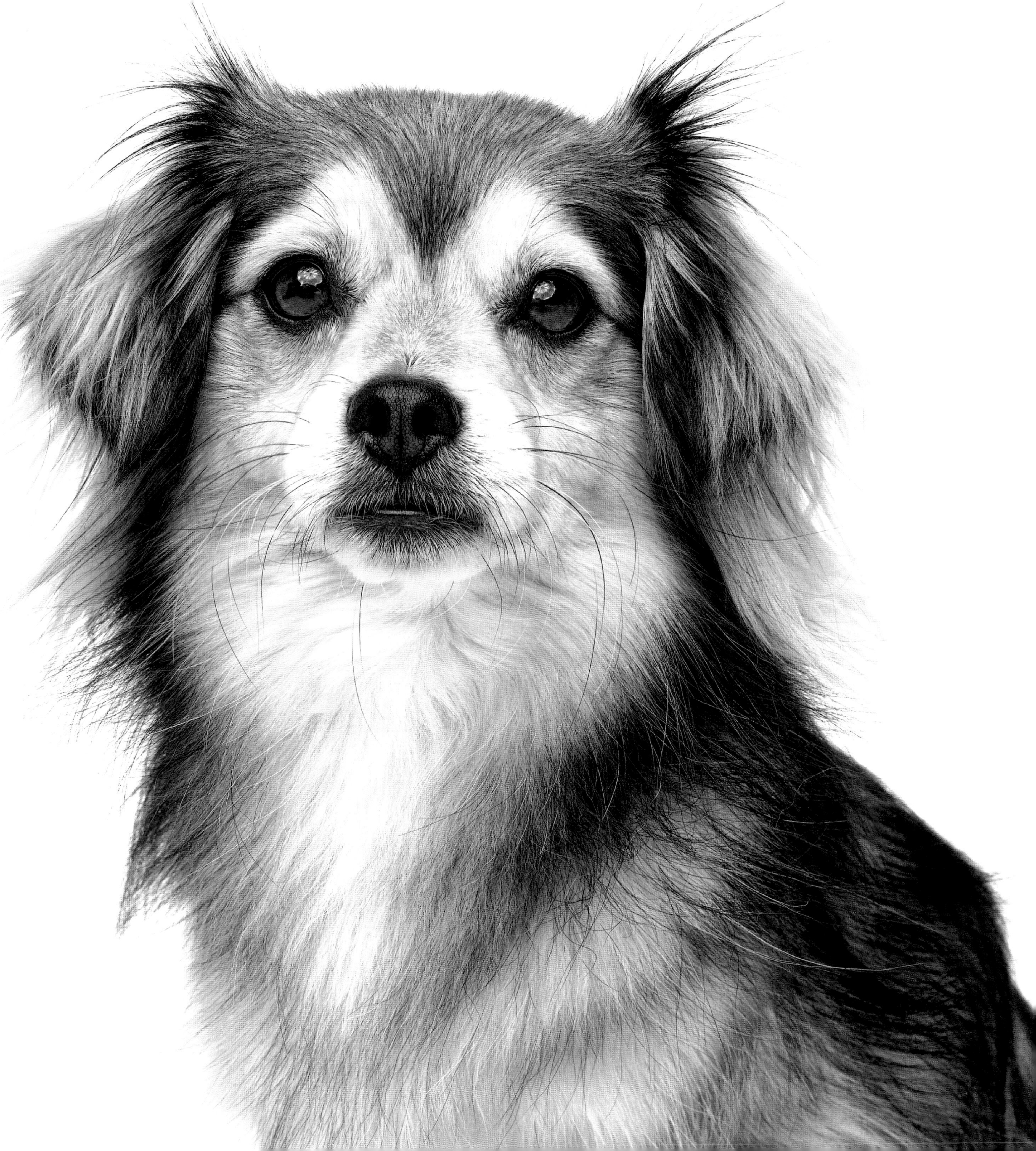

Champ & Suzie Q

Izzy & Cassie

Arlo & Sailor

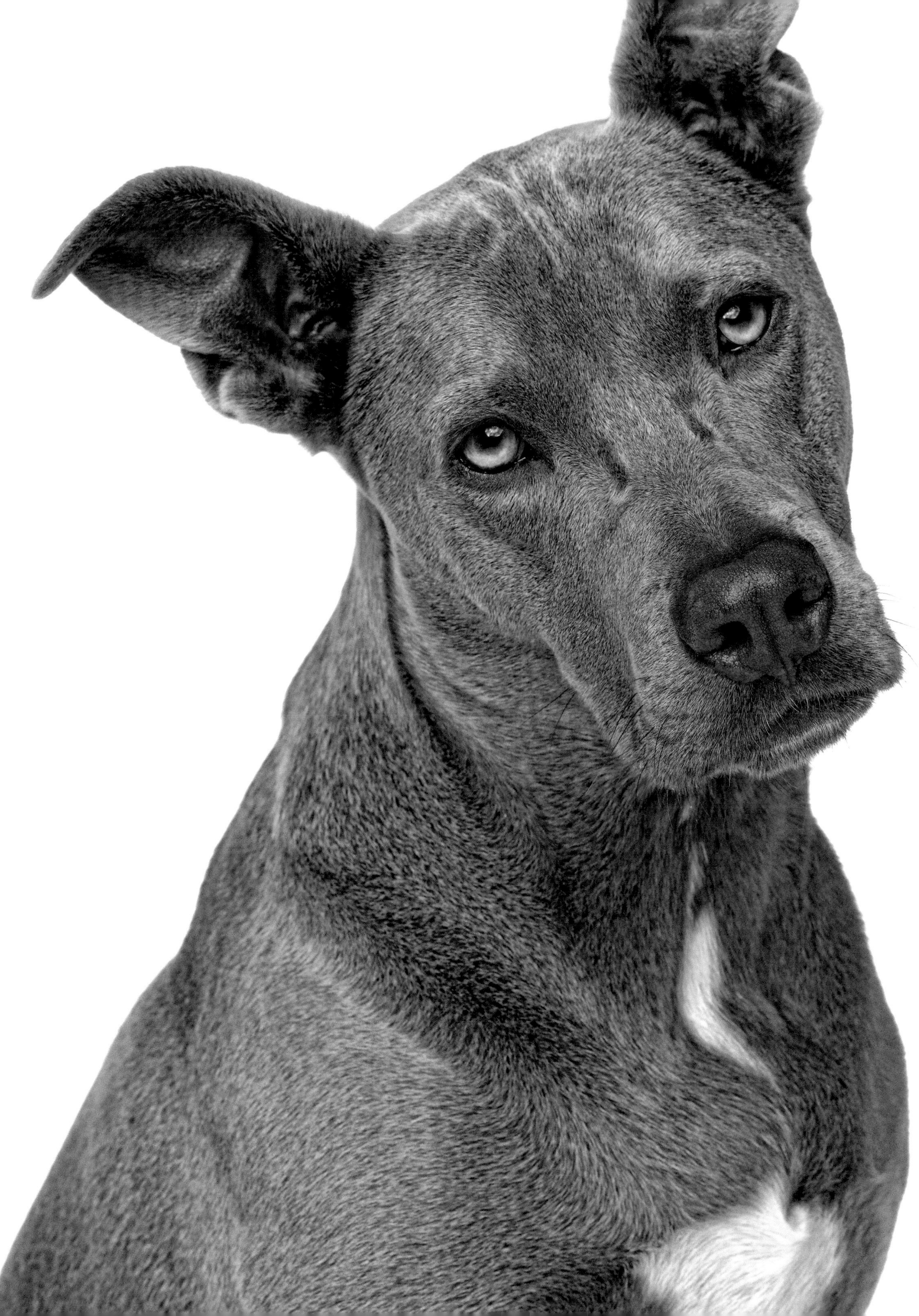

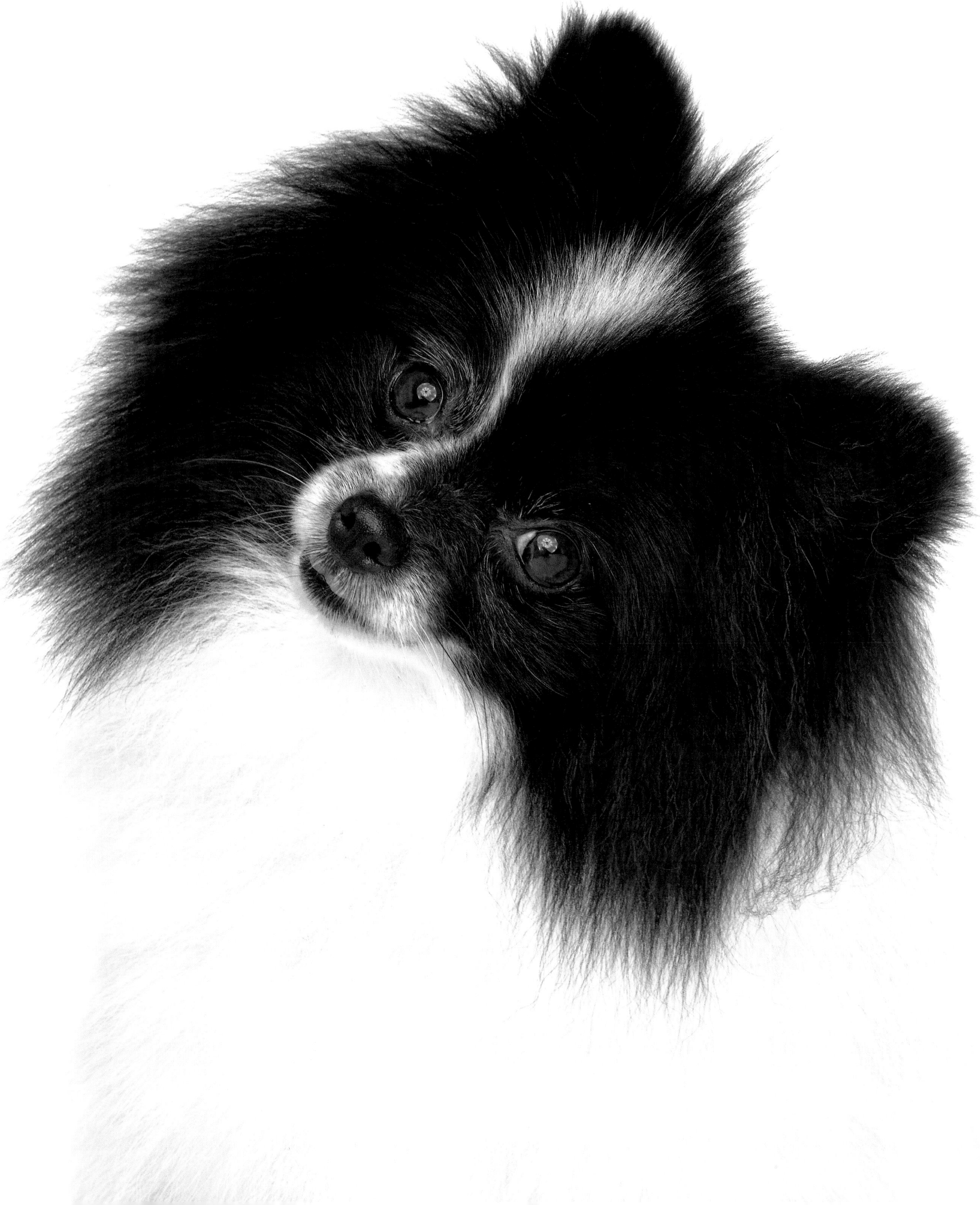

Panda & Big Shot

Bella & Spike

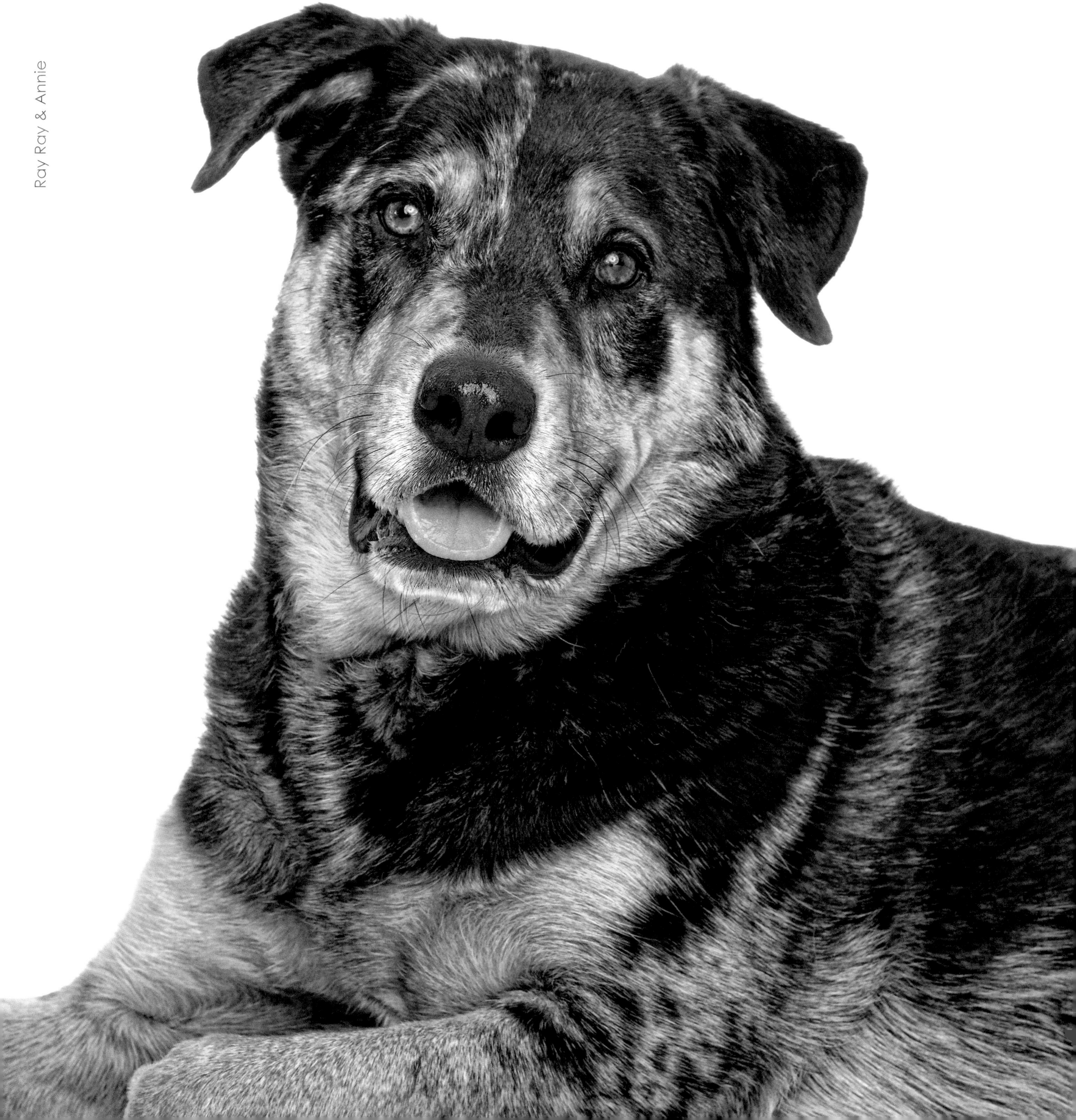

Ray Ray & Annie

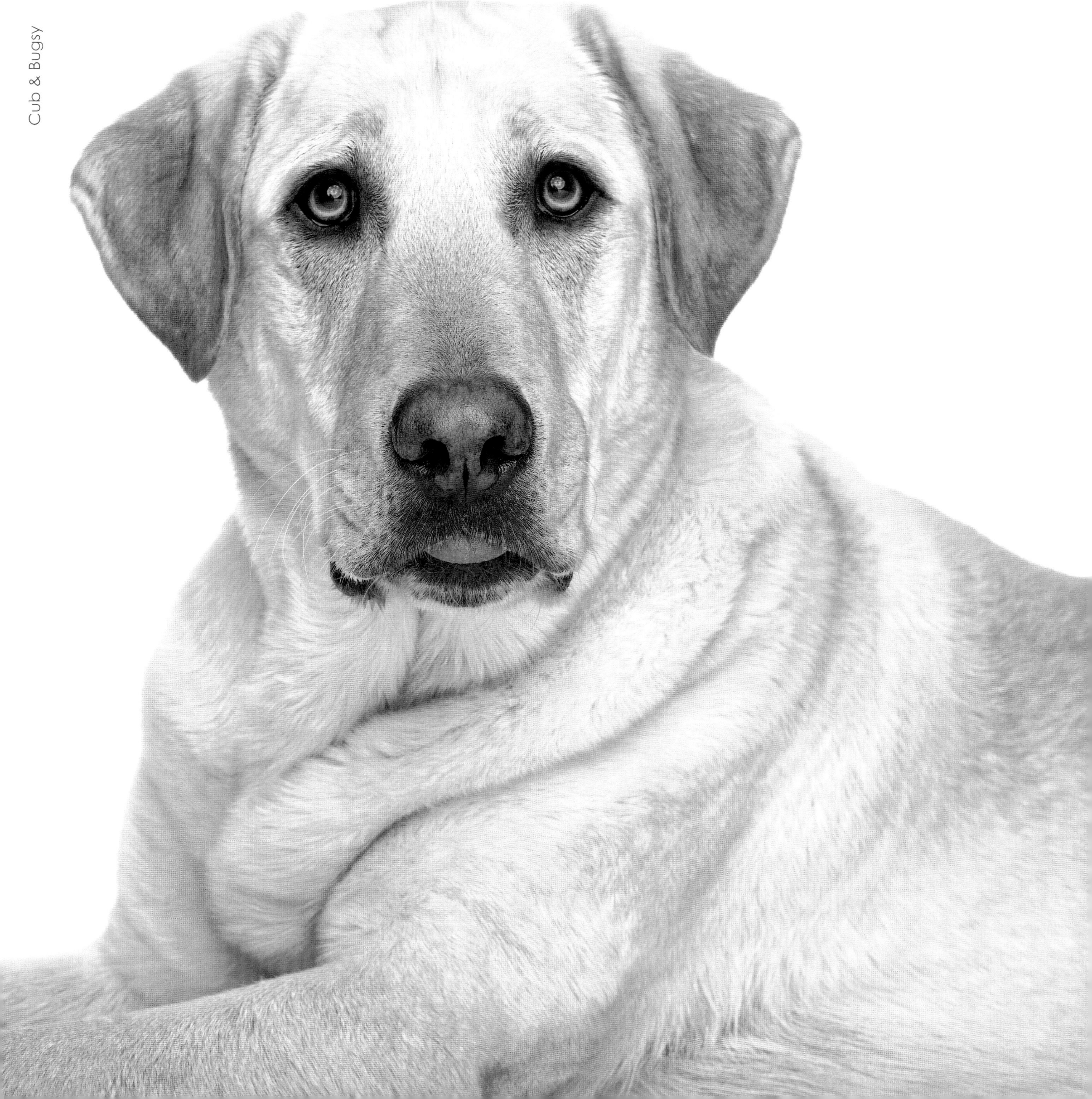

Cub & Bugsy

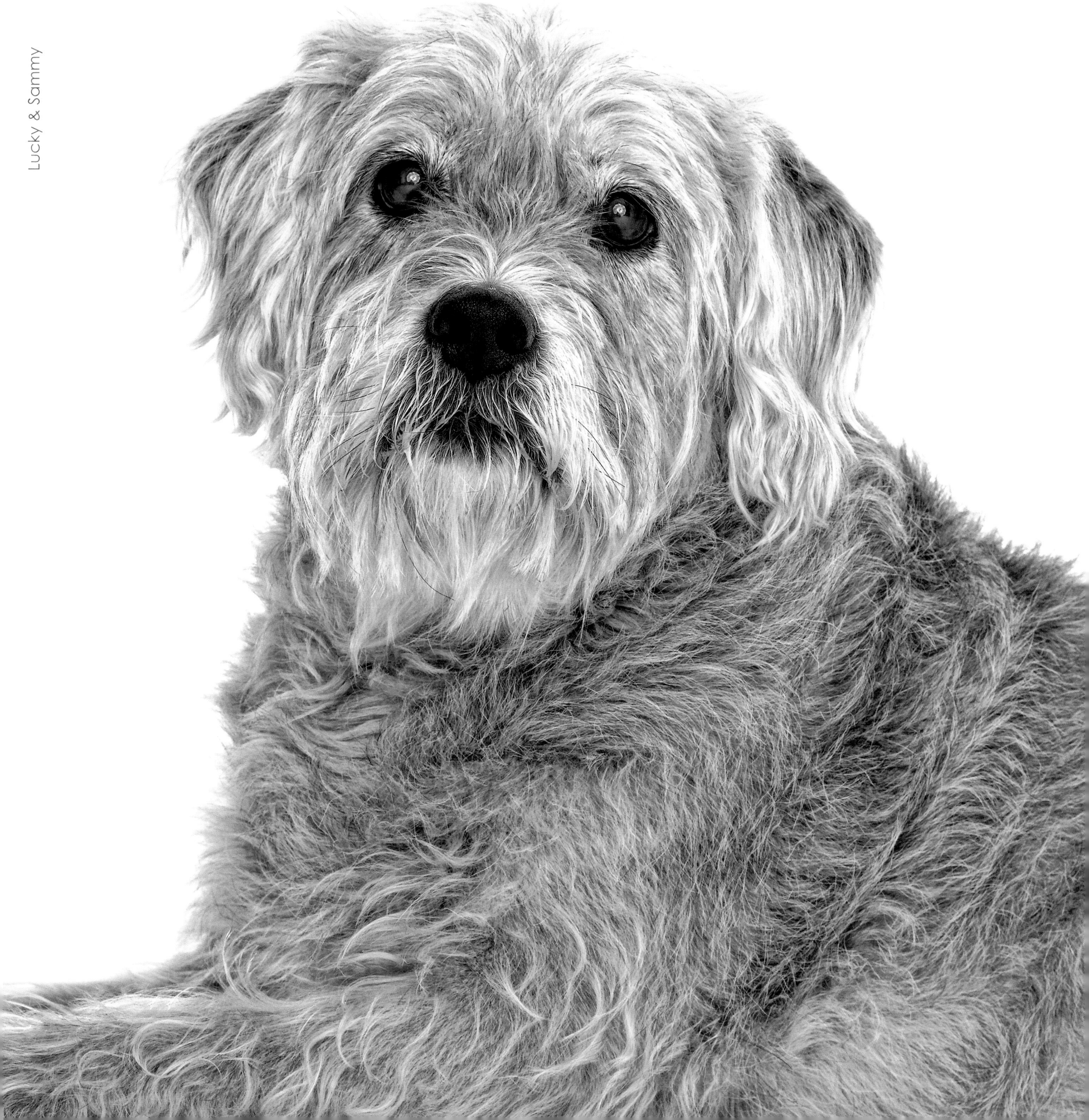

Lucky & Sammy

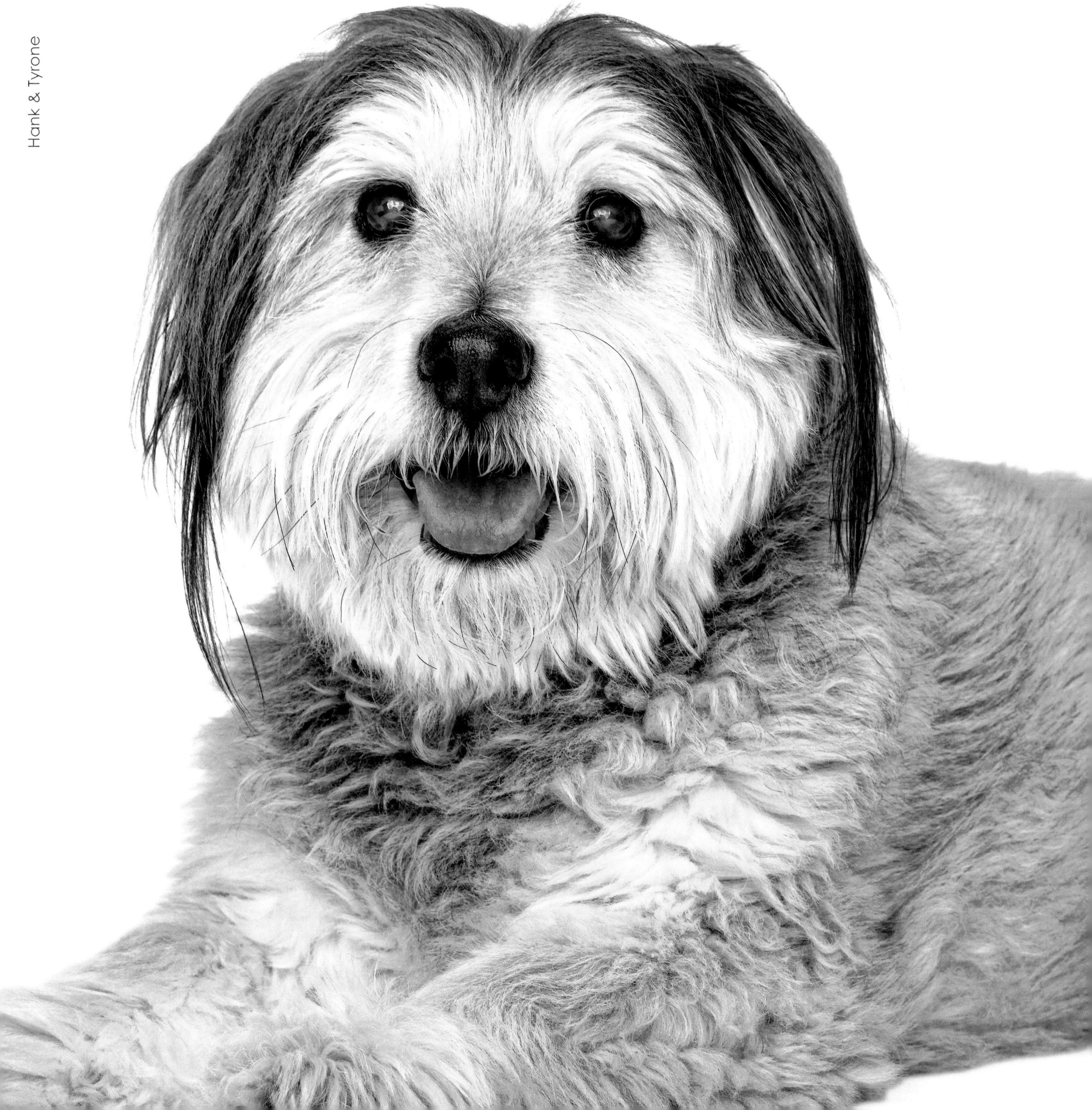

Hank & Tyrone

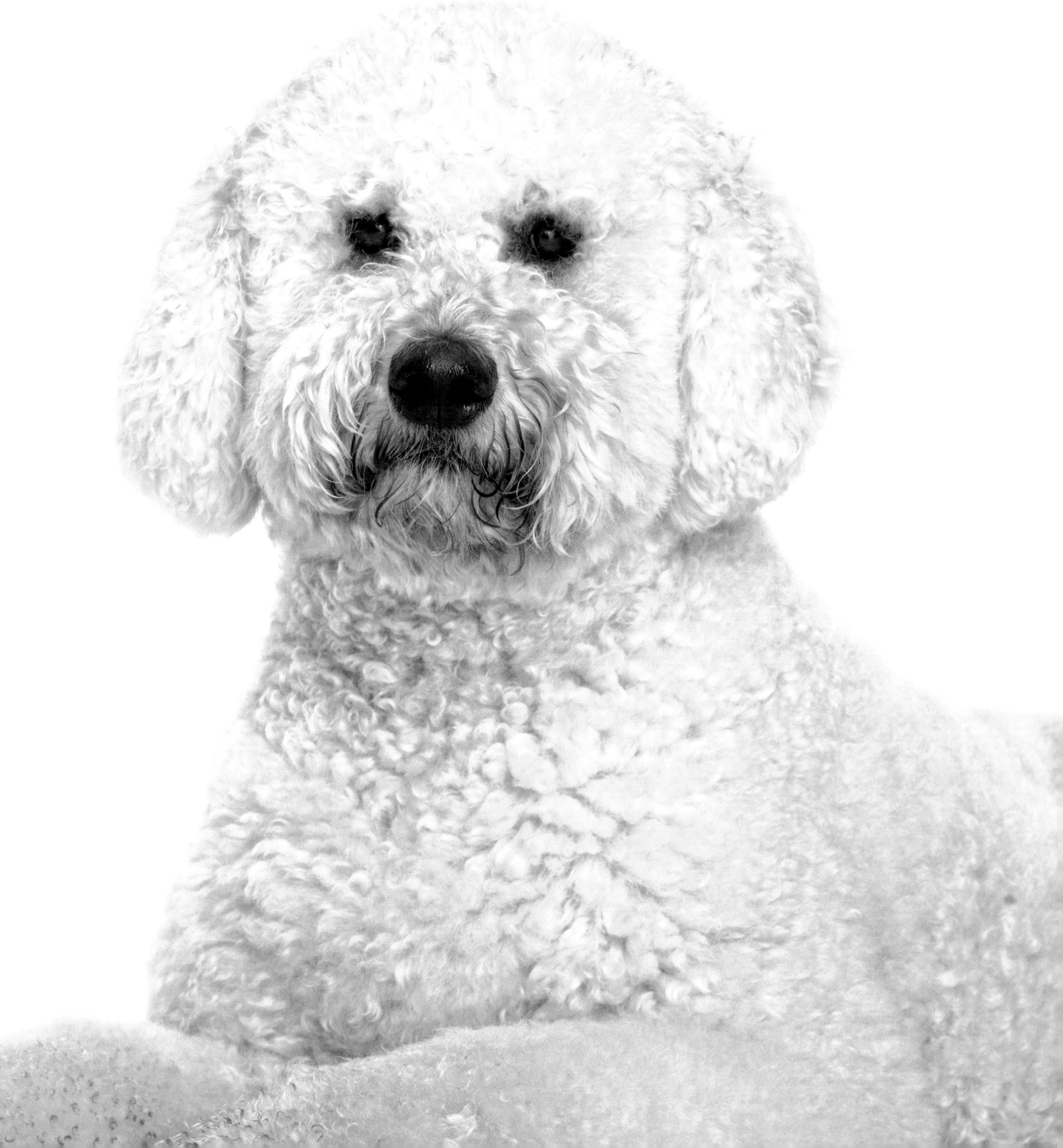

Marley & Rufus

Yogi & Eloise

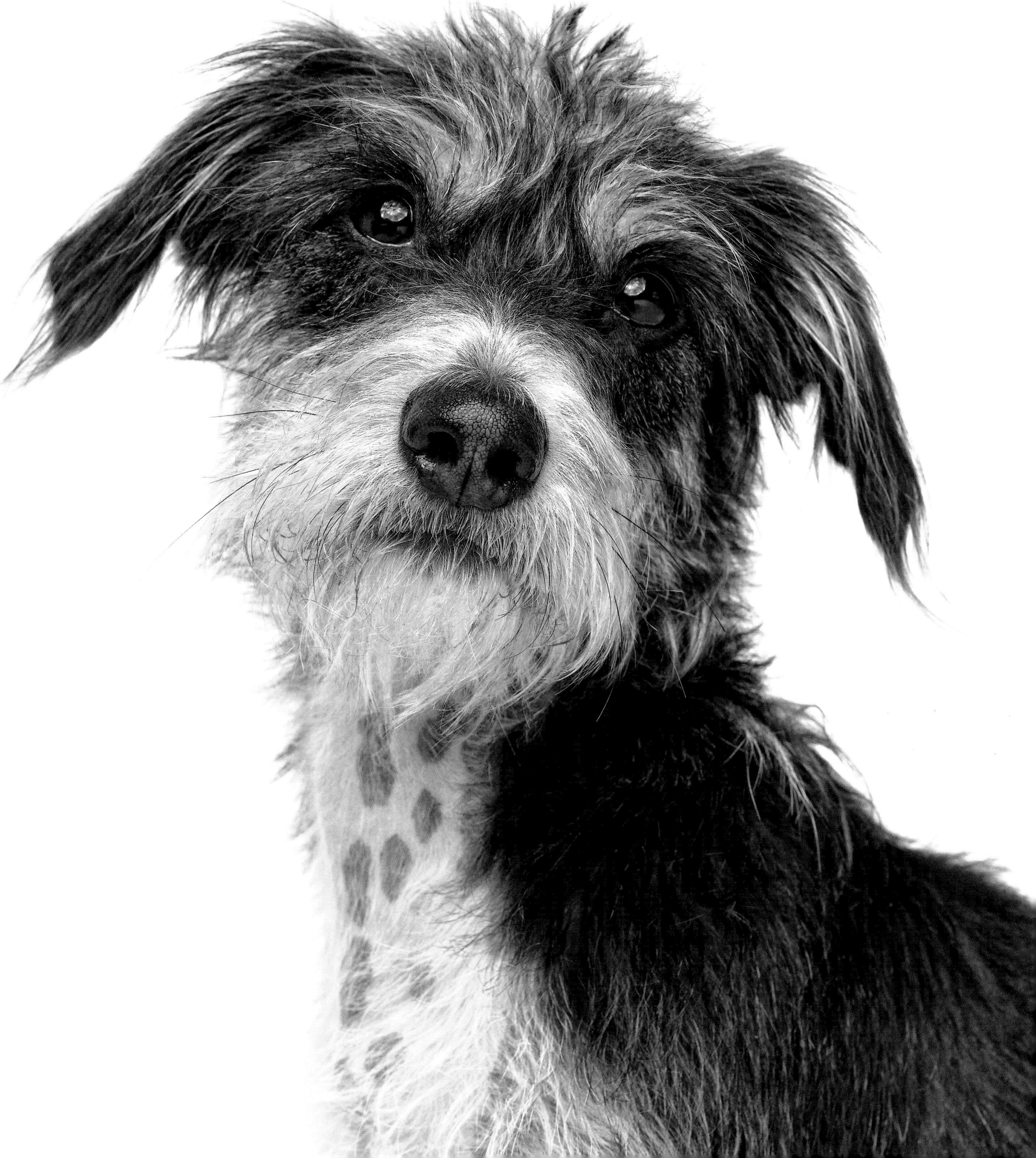

Sawyer & Poppy

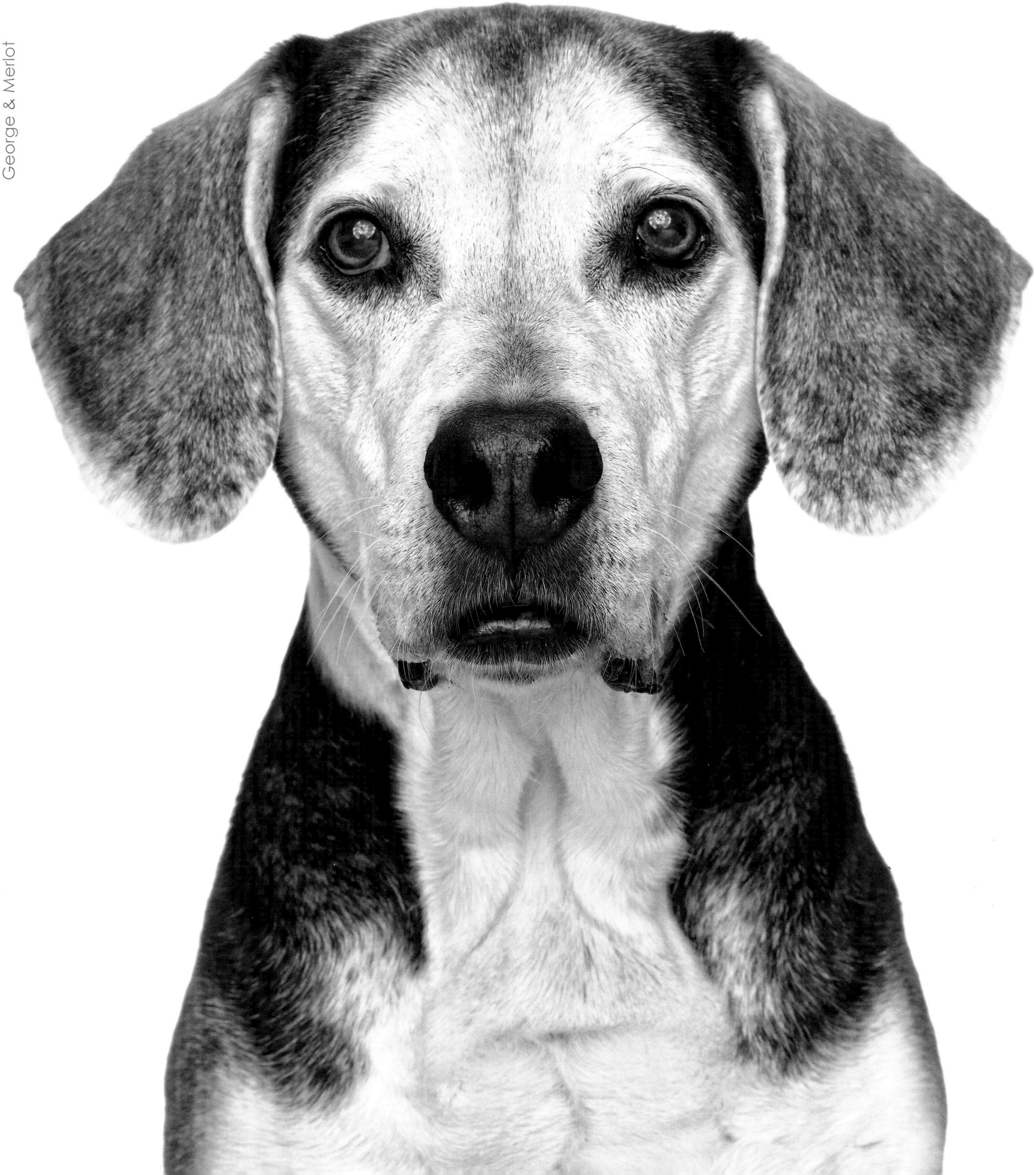

George & Merlot

Charley & Lola

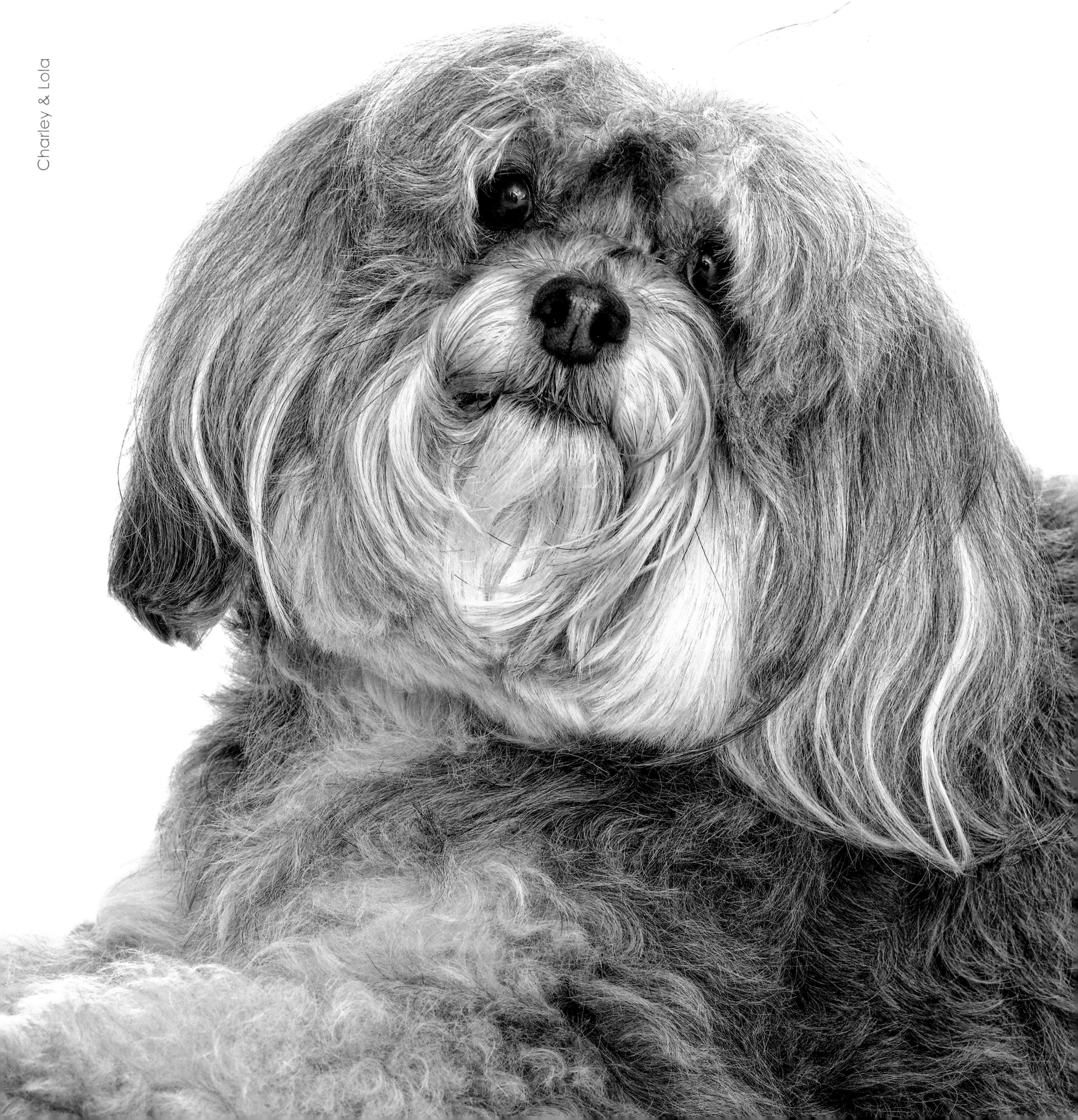

Leo

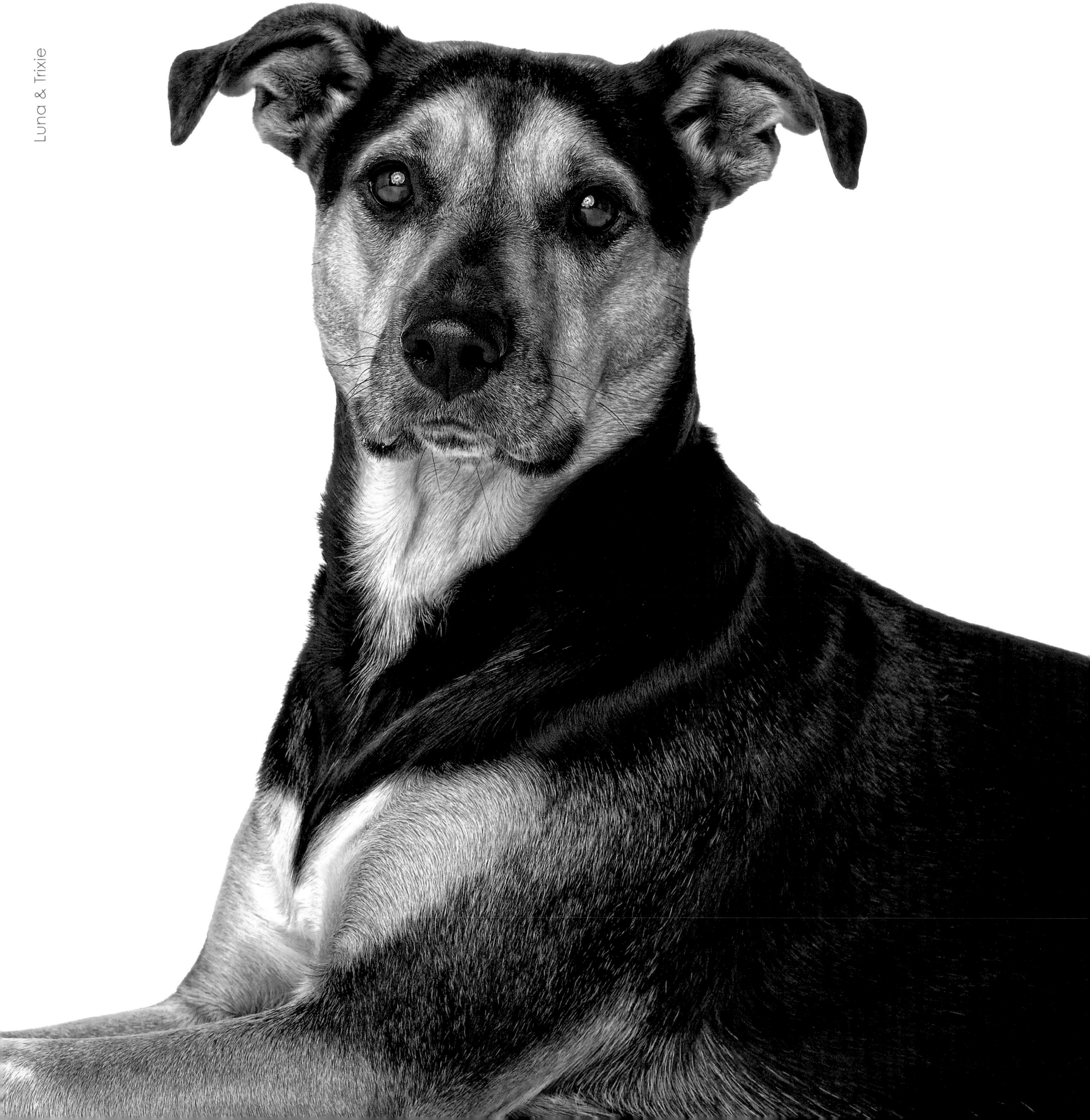

Luna & Trixie

Riley

Ria & Max

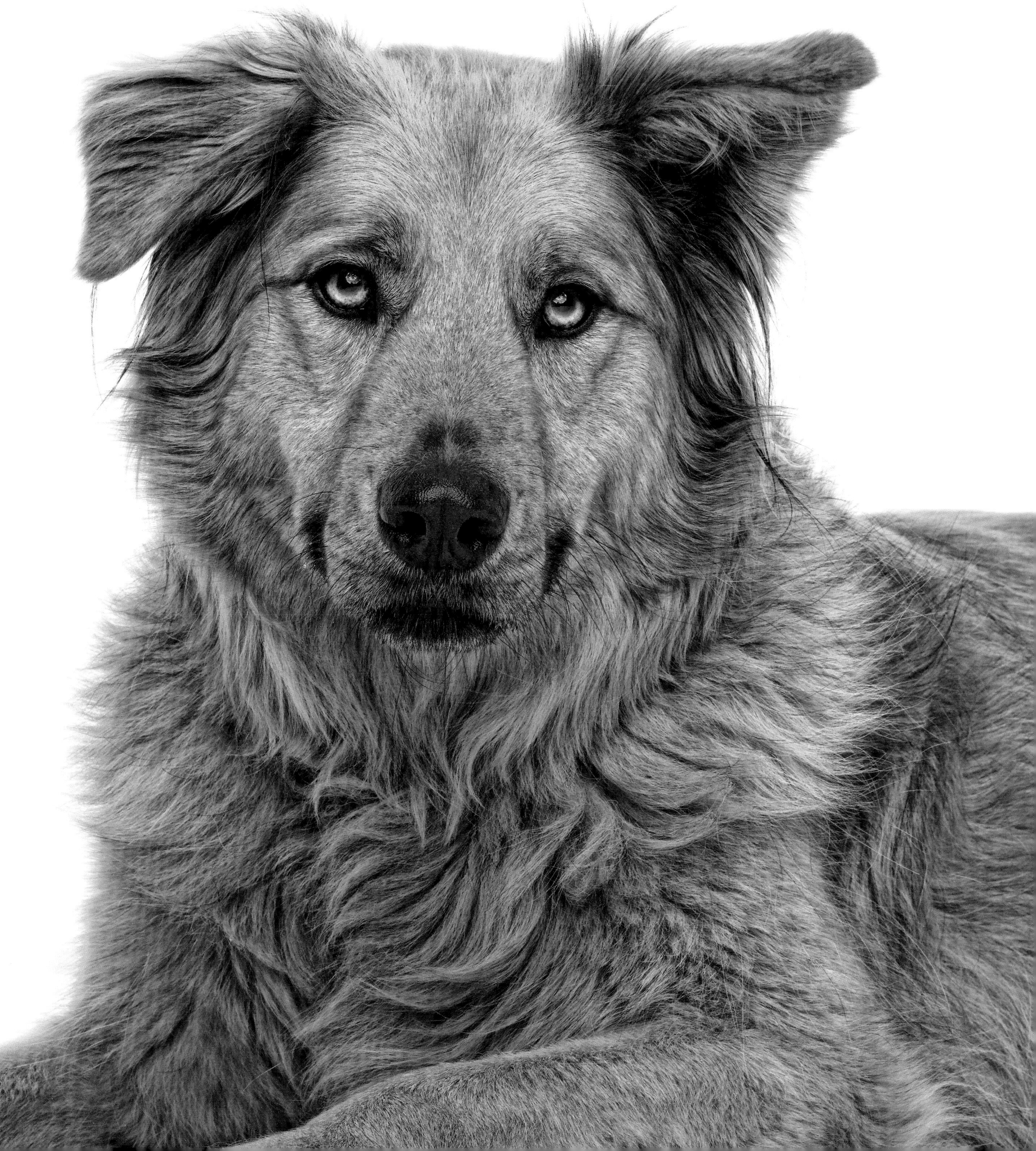

Gulliver & Shammy

Lola & Gracie Mae

Beau

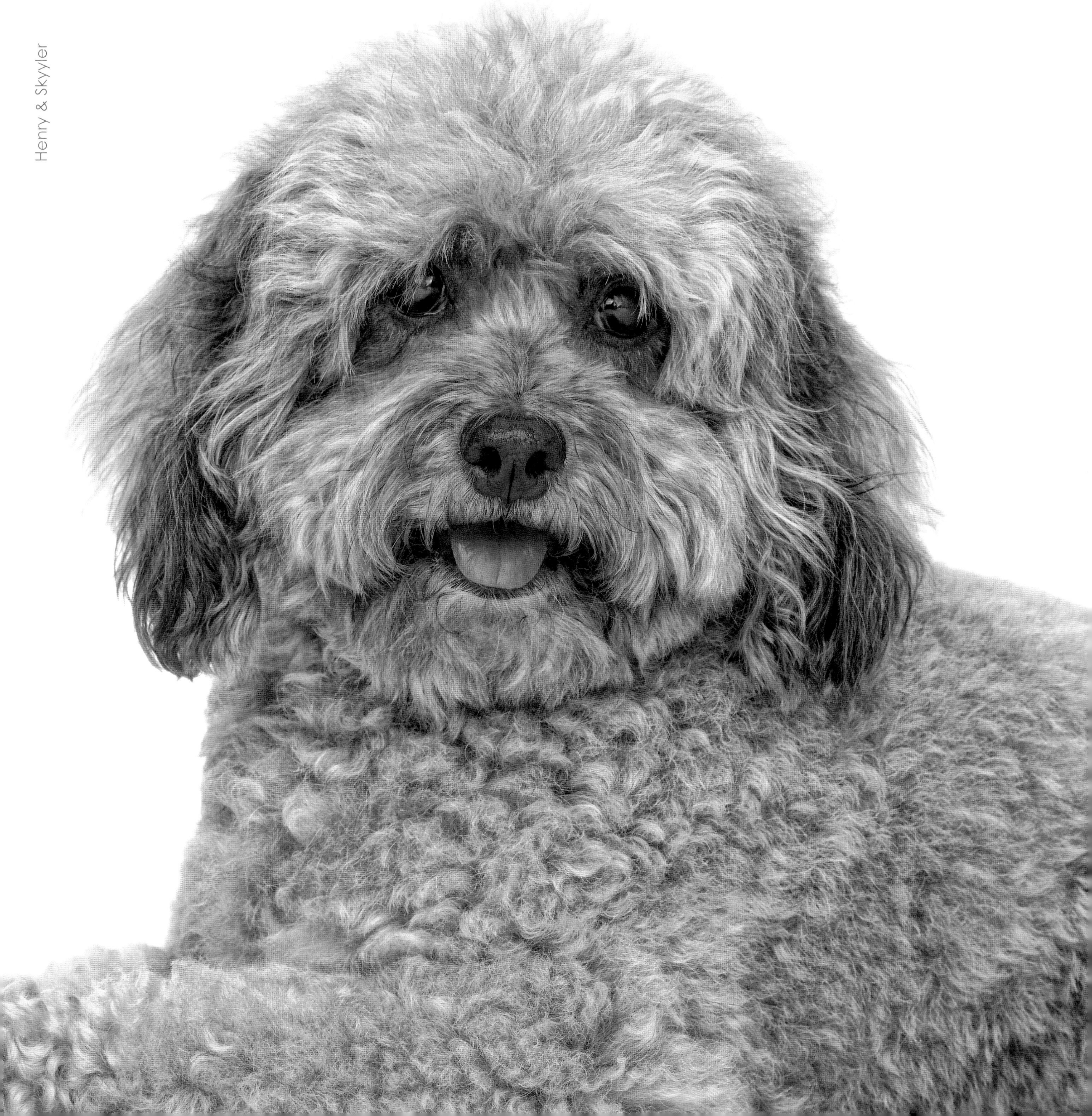

Henry & Skyyler

Twinkee & Bentley

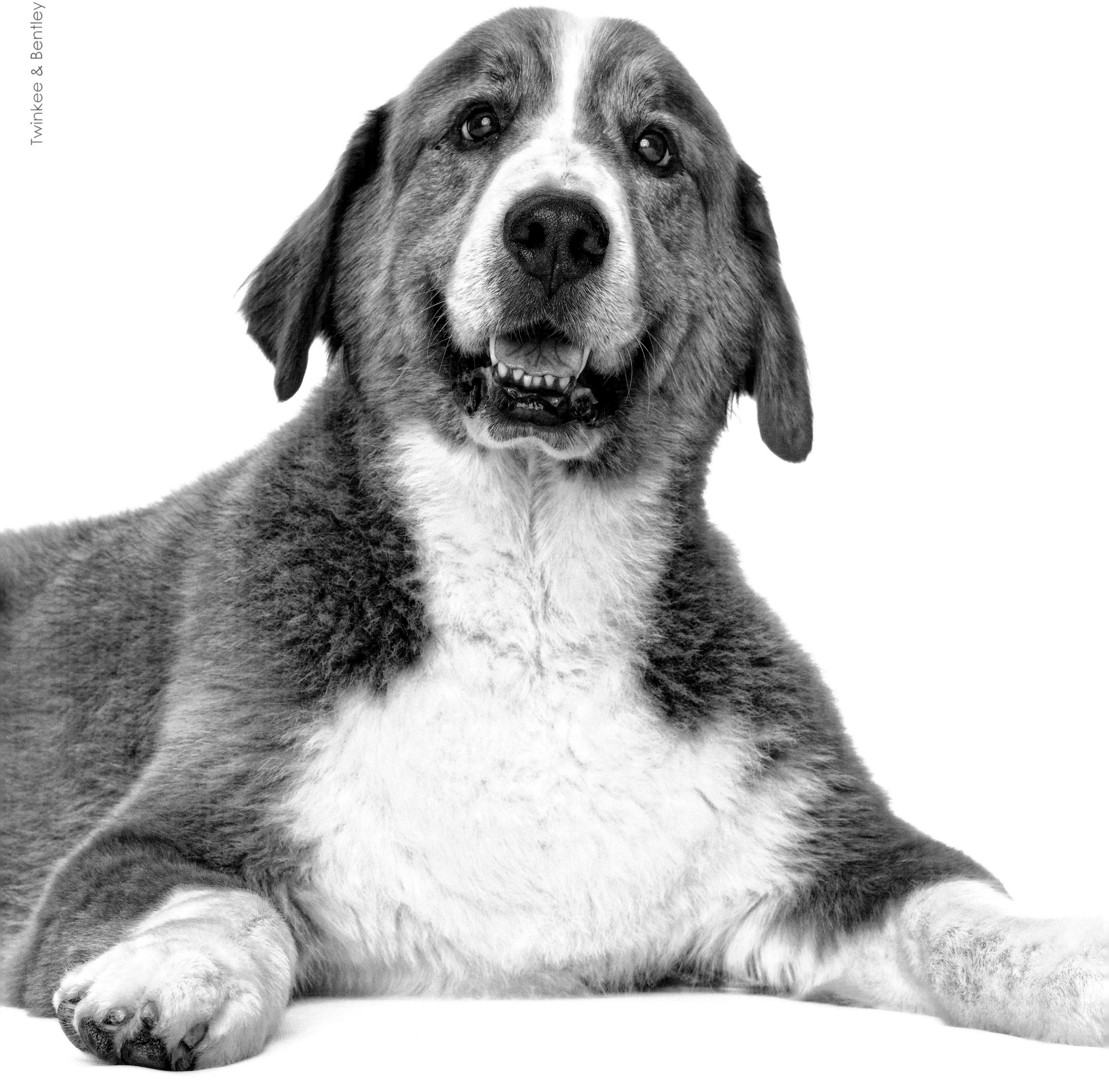

Axel & Brody

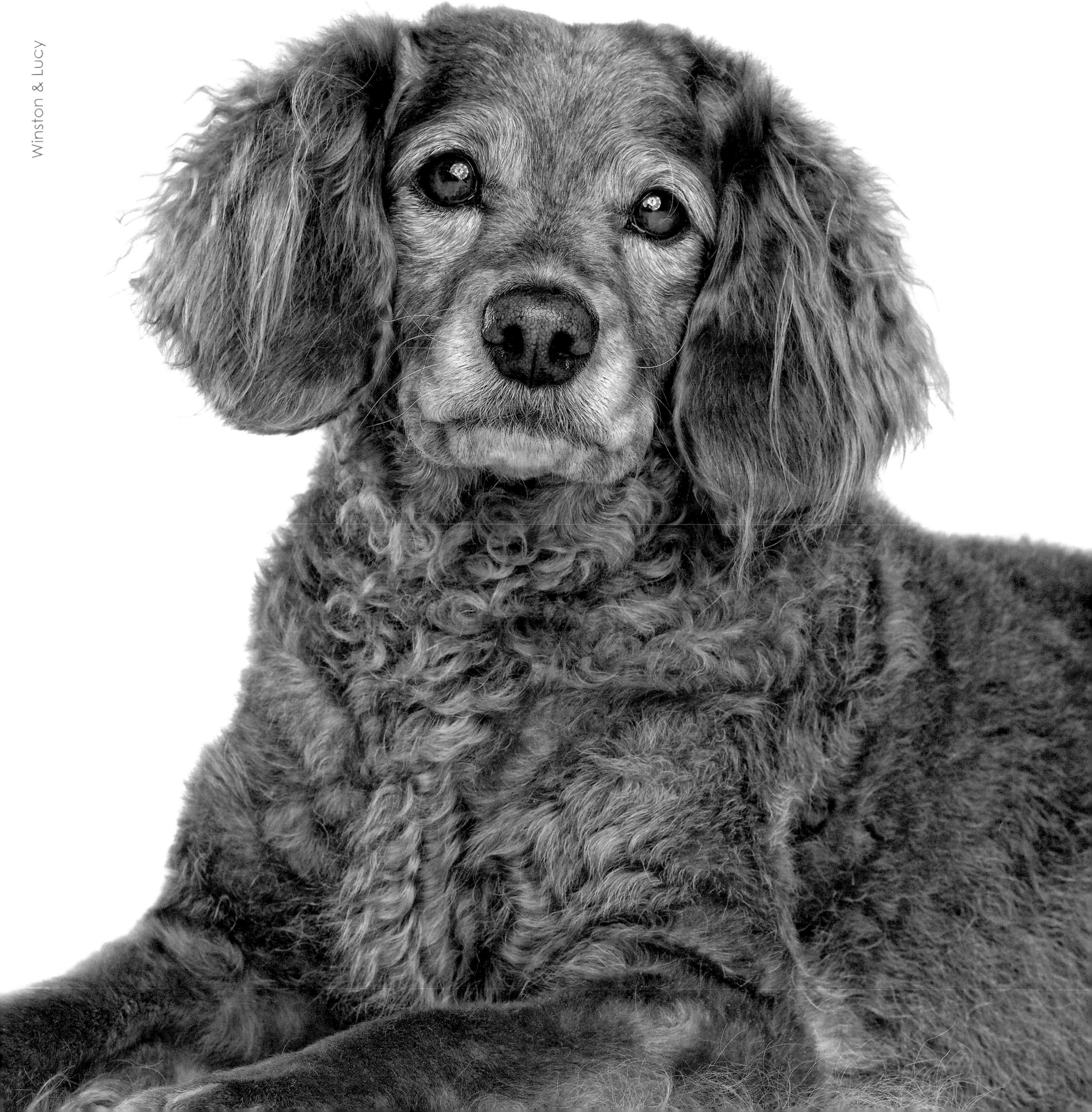

Winston & Lucy

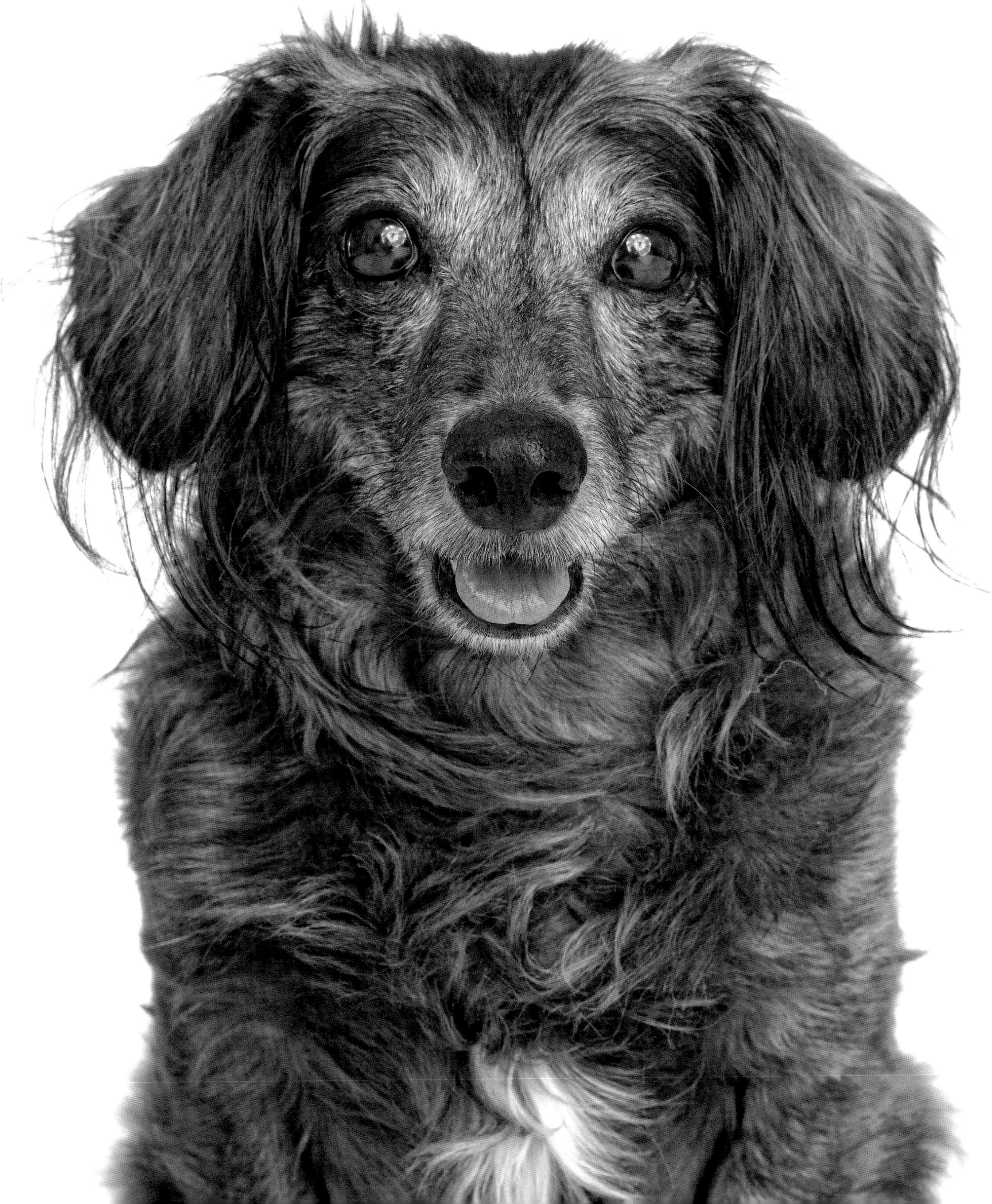

Jonas & Sebastian

Nala

The Rover Story

By Andrew Grant

I've always loved animals, especially dogs and cats. While producing *Rover*, my parents told the story of how I begged for a dog for months and months when I was a first grader. When my father came home with a goldfish, my response was, "You can't hug a goldfish, Dad." Days later, they took me to a shelter where we adopted a dog I named "Benji." Benji was a great dog, but barked. A LOT. I recall a doorbell once interrupting Benji's dinner and my frustrated Mother scolding, "Benji, don't bark with your mouth full!"

Benji, like most dogs, had full reign over the house, but she wasn't allowed in the front living room and especially not on the "fancy" furniture. We regularly found evidence of Benji's visits to that room while the family was away. Fur on the couch and cushions warm to the touch were dead giveaways, but Benji would never confess to the transgressions. One day, the family piled into the car and drove off to church. Everyone, except for me. I hid quietly in the closet in the adjacent foyer and peered through the louvers in the door. Minutes later, and just as I had predicted, I spied Benji strolling into the living room, hopping up on the couch and curling up in a ball for a relaxing nap. I opened the door, snapped a picture of Benji on the forbidden bed and laughed. I still have that photo today. The expression on his face is clear. "Fine. You caught me. I'm guilty. Congratulations. Now would you mind leaving me alone so I can get some rest?" That all happened nearly 30 years ago, but we all still laugh about it today. Those are the fun and memorable moments pets bring to our lives. They truly become part of the family, and the void they leave behind when they're gone is profound.

We are truly blessed to have animals here with us. They enrich our lives in so many ways. They make us laugh. They provide us with companionship. They give us a sense of purpose. They protect us. They have an uncanny ability to provide comfort when we need it most. But most of all, they show us what it means to love unconditionally. But we can't forget that they're just innocent animals that depend on us to provide them with food, care and shelter. It is our responsibility to take care of them, and we're failing them. Millions of them.

In 2009, I had an idea to produce an art book of dogs after including two dogs in a photograph for an advertisement for Chef Works in San Diego. After I learned about the staggering number of cats and dogs that are euthanized each and every year, I was compelled to act. I began production of the first *Rover* book just two weeks later. I did so without having done any research on book publishing or looking at other dog books. I just knew this was something I should do as I knew I could bring attention to the tragedy.

I never photographed a dog in the studio before, and I put my first subject, a large husky (right on following page) on a large table with a rather slippery surface. He slid around and didn't seem very comfortable. I quickly determined I would have to photograph the dogs while lying on the floor with them. The first few shoots were very difficult, and I didn't capture many compelling shots, as I had very little experience working with dogs and knew very little about training them. Eventually, I learned how to make my subjects more comfortable and how to elicit and capture compelling expressions that captures their diverse personalities. During the next six months, I photographed about 100 dogs for the first 300-page book and spent hundreds of hours preparing images and designing the book. At first, it seemed impossible to complete a book in just a few months, but

Merlot

I had an incredible amount of serendipity in my life when I began production of the first book. Everything I needed to produce the book seemed to fall directly in my lap. So much so that I was able to manifest an idea into a book in just six months. I had the idea for the book in February of 2009, began photographing dogs in March, finished preparing the images and designing the book in August, performed color press checks in September, and the book was featured on the *Ellen DeGeneres Show* in December. That serendipity remains in my life today and is a constant reminder that I'm on the right path.

During the last five years, I've spent about 1,000 hours photographing 600 dogs and thousands of hours preparing the images for print, designing the books, organizing fund raisers and promoting the books. It's a tremendous amount of work, but it's worth it. I've watched and listened to people as they flip through the books. I've seen how people react to the dogs' faces, and I'm certain *Rover* has inspired many people to help rescue pets.

Every year, millions of cats and dogs enter pet shelters and rescues in the United States. I believe they must feel lost, displaced and alone when they're living in a rescue. Many of the dogs I visit at rescues seem scared and sad in their cages despite extraordinary efforts made by most rescues to make them as comfortable as possible. I've photographed many dogs living in rescues. It's a bittersweet experience. Some of them will sprint out of the kennel area to wherever I may be leading them. After a few moments of play in the studio they come out of their shell and their true personality is revealed. After we've captured the shots we need, it's time to take them back to their cage. It's often a struggle and always heartbreaking. It's clear to me that all of them want nothing more than someone to love and somewhere to call home.

Most of the dogs inside these pages, including the purebreds, once lived in a rescue or shelter. Some of the dogs were living in a rescue when they were photographed and remain there today. Some of the dogs were rescued after being discarded on the streets. Some of the dogs were surrendered after their family lost their home to foreclosure. One of the dogs, "Hero," was once used as "bait" for dog fighting. After years of gentle and patient care, he's a happy, playful, trusting soul.

Some of the *Rover* dogs are cared for by pet advocates who made a generous donation to have their dog photographed and featured in the pages of *Rover*. This program generated donations of over $1,000,000 to rescues we selected across the country. Immortalizing one's best friend in a popular book is an extraordinarily unique opportunity. As a result, the rescues we've selected to benefit are able to use *Rover* as a vehicle to attract new donors who weren't familiar with the rescue's efforts in the community. The fact that many donors will continue to support worthy organizations for many years is the most rewarding part of the project for us.

Finally, some of the dogs in the *Rover* books were rescued literally minutes before they were scheduled to be euthanized. Each and every time I see their pictures, I am struck by the fact that their precious experience of life was nearly ended years ago, simply because nobody offered to give them a home. There are absolutely beautiful, smart, fun, healthy purebreds and mixed breeds available for adoption at rescues. I hope the grateful and loving faces inside will inspire you to welcome a shelter pet into your home.

Visit RoverToTheRescue.com to learn how you can help rescues and to watch our progress.

Argent

Rover to the Rescue

Let's be heros!

QUICK! Think of a hero. Spandex. Fluttering cape. White horse and shining armor. A gold badge. A firefighter's hat. That's what most people think of when they consider "heroes." But that's just one way of defining heroism. Whoever said there was only one way to be a hero? Whoever said that all heroes need to dodge bullets and leap tall buildings?

Heroism is about courage. Not necessarily courage to save the world, but the courage to do something for the good of others. To help others who can't help themselves. To have the desire to make a difference when the status quo is not tolerable. To take the initiative in creating new means for change when conventional routes don't apply. To take the first small step toward making a bigger difference. In fact, that's what drove a photographer to do something to try to make a difference and create *Rover*.

Every hero has an origin story

It all started with a camera. Andrew Grant, an acclaimed commercial photographer, was shooting an ad campaign and catalog for Chef Works at a Bulthaup kitchen showroom when the owner's two French bulldogs, Gaston and Napoleon, kept wandering into the picture. Rather than ask the gracious owner of the store to keep her dogs away from the busy set, Andrew was captivated by what he saw through the lens and recognized an opportunity. At the end of the day, some of the most evocative and winning shots were of the dogs at the centerpiece. Andrew enjoyed working with the dogs so much, he started thinking about someday making a photo book of dogs.

"Well, 'someday' quickly became next week, when I learned just how many dogs and cats enter shelters every year and the dramatic effect the recession and housing crisis were having on rescues. There was an immediate sense of urgency, as I knew a book like this could bring attention to the crisis."

Andrew was flabbergasted by the statistics. To him, they painted a tragic picture almost more compelling than the pictures he had taken of the dogs. He thought back to his childhood friend Benji, a shelter dog his family adopted as a boy, and became committed to bringing this vision to life. He knew that with his expertise and connections, he could, in his own small way, create something of significant impact.

A camera led to a book

Producing the *Rover* books is a monumental task. On average, Andrew spends approximately two hours with each dog to get "the shots." Some dogs take only minutes, but it sometimes takes hours to get just two solid shots of less cooperative, shy or timid dogs. Andrew personally edits the images, discarding any shots that aren't "razor sharp" or compelling. Andrew then meticulously cleans up and prepares hundreds of images for the book in Adobe Photoshop®, a task that takes approximately four months to complete. Each of the more than 500 images reveal his incredible commitment to bringing the books to life. With each lovingly crafted photograph in *Rover*, he hopes to inspire others to make their own contribution toward helping shelter animals.

Listen up...

Every year, **millions** of cats and dogs enter pet rescues and shelters in the United States.

Over 56% dogs and puppies
entering shelters are euthanized every year.

An estimated **4 million** cats and dogs are euthanized every year.

That's approximately 1 death every **8 seconds.**

Sources: National Council on Pet Population Study, The Humane Society of the United States

Stewy

How you can help

Everyday heroes

Rover to the Rescue is rooted in the belief that small actions can make a big impact and that the combined efforts of many people can lead to significant change. We believe this to be true because *Rover* itself is the result of a small action. It was a small action that became a book, which then became a brand that animal-lovers rally around. And now it has become more than a brand, but a call to action and a banner for change. From one small book to a full-fledged rescue effort — we are Rover to the Rescue!

We are seeking Everyday Heroes. Not just pet owners. Not even animal rescuers. These are people who, when looking through the *Rover* book, see more than a collection of furry friends. They see true companions and recognize in their open gazes a sense of hope and longing, of expectation and pure joy.

More importantly, these are people who feel compelled to do something — a small-business owner looking to partner with the Rover to the Rescue brand or someone just wanting to be part of a worthy cause. Regardless of who they are or what they do, we invite them to join us in helping dogs.

And not just help us help dogs. We want them to help dogs themselves. However, they can, whenever they can, wherever they can. We want them to be a champion for good by contributing in their own way. We want them to be a leader for progress by making that first small step toward a larger impact. We are looking for others to aid the cause. We are looking for others to come to the rescue. We are calling upon those who don't just want to make a difference — but forge their own path and actually create one. Are you an everyday hero?

Be heroic! Small actions lead to big impact

There are many ways you can raise money and bring awareness to rescues. Collectively, our efforts will help countless cats and dogs find a loving home. Visit RoverToTheRescue.com to learn how you can become a hero to homeless pets.

Our mission

Our goal is to help reduce euthanizations and the rescue pet population by supporting spaying and neutering programs, dispelling myths about shelter pets and inspiring people to welcome a homeless pet into their home.

1. Support organizations which have a comprehensive spaying and neutering program in place.

2. Promote the importance of spaying and neutering, and support those efforts.

3. Dispell myths about shelter animals.

4. Promote that there are healthy, smart and beautiful purebreds and mixed breeds available at rescues.

How we help rescues

Rover has generated donations of over $1,000,000 for rescues across the country
Rover visits several rescues in each community and selects one deserving rescue to support. We primarily support organizations which already have comprehensive spaying and neutering programs in place. Chosen rescues are able to use their exclusive partnership with *Rover* as a vehicle to bring awareness to their organization and attract new donors. Secondly, because most of the dogs featured in *Rover* once lived in a rescue or shelter, we discredit the stigma of shelter pets by beautifully illustrating that there are smart, healthy, fun, loving dogs available for adoption everywhere. Finally, *Rover* media coverage enables selected rescues to highlight their services, generate donations, recruit volunteers in the community and place pets in forever homes.

Providing rescues with a way to attract new donors
Selected rescues are able to present prospective and existing donors with an extraordinary and exclusive opportunity to immortalize their dog in a book. We take great pride in the fact that *Rover* is used by deserving rescues to attract new donors, bridge new relationships and get existing donors involved.

Animal Rescue Fund of the Hamptons, Wainscott, NY • Corridor Rescue, Houston, TX • Eagle Vail Humane Society, Eagle, CO • Friends of Animals Utah, Park City, UT • Dog Adoption and Welfare Group, Santa Barbara, CA • Dogs Without Borders, Los Angeles, CA • Happy Tales Humane, Franklin, TN • Hawaiian Island Humane Society, Kailua Kona, HI • Humane Society of Broward County, Fort Lauderdale, CA • Humane Society of South Coastal Georgia, Brunswick, GA • Lucky Day Animal Rescue, Aspen, CO • New Leash on Life, Los Angeles, CA • New York City Animal Care and Control, New York, NY • Operation Kindness, Dallas, TX • PAWS, Chicago, IL • PAWS, Jackson Hole, WY • Pets Unlimited of San Francisco, CA • Providence Animal Rescue League, Providence, RI • Second Chance Rescue, Ridgway, CO • Shelter of Wood River Valley, Sun Valley, ID • Rancho Coastal Humane Society, San Diego, CA • Rescue Me Dog, Saratoga, WY • Washington Animal Rescue League, Washington, DC • We Care Animal Rescue, St. Helena, CA, Spot, Los Angeles, CA

How *Rover* can help your rescue
Visit RoverToTheRescue.com to discover how we can help raise money for your organization.

results of our

online survey

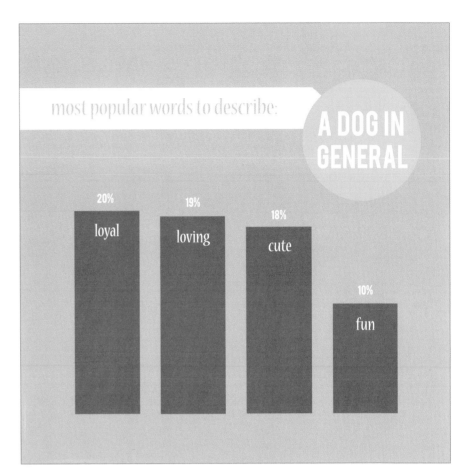

most popular words to describe:

A DOG IN GENERAL

20% loyal
19% loving
18% cute
10% fun

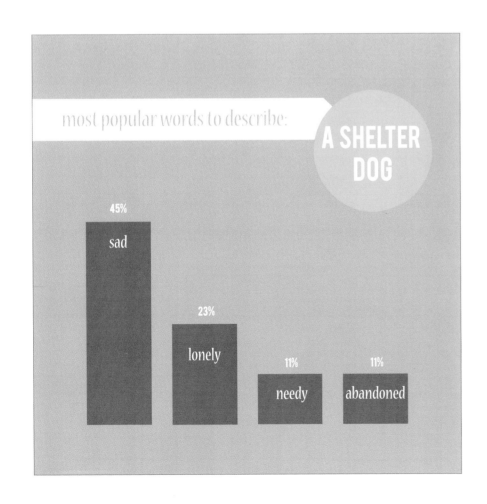

most popular words to describe:

A SHELTER DOG

45% sad
23% lonely
11% needy
11% abandoned

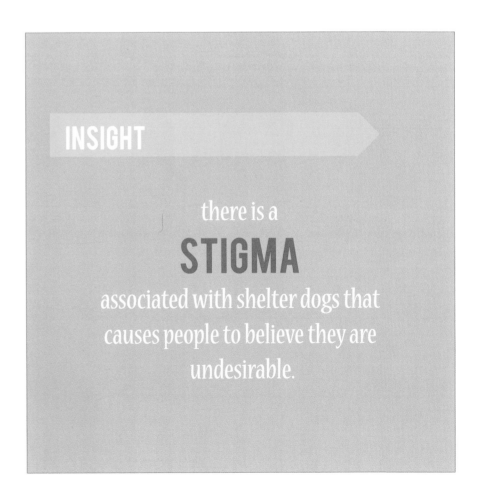

INSIGHT

there is a

STIGMA

associated with shelter dogs that causes people to believe they are undesirable.

Joe

Rover donors

These generous and caring people helped Rover to the Rescue generate donations of over one million dollars to rescues across the country.

Lynn & Ted Leonsis, Jill Schulz Transki, Marti & Wayne Huizenga, Wayne Jr. & Fonda Huizenga, Jennifer & Ray Huizenga, Steve & Jeannie Hudson, Pam & Jay Alexander, Scott & Holly Bodenweber, Heidi Klum, Stacey Gerrish & The Kaufman Family Foundation, Dave & Nadine Lipson, The Wasserman Foundation, Mindy Weiss & Robert David, Judy & Mark D. Lerner, Debbie Attanasio, Haven & Mike Parchinski, Leah & Sam Fischer, Jerrod Blandino & Too Faced Cosmetics, Nicole & Steve Finger, Diane & Michael Ziering, Kathryn & Harry Peisach, Richard & Kitza Goodman, Cheryl Bressler, Barbara & Mark Lemmon, Derek & Sophie Craighead, Liz Levitt-Hirsch, Nicola & Wally Opdycke, Mac & Mary Kay Mcinnis, Jamie & Terry Stiles, Doreen Koenig, Jackie Whitley, Donna Skeen, Marei Von Saher, Charlène von Saher, Patricia Yarberry Allen M.D. & Douglas A. Mcintrye, Ann & Tom Unterberg, Holly & Bill James, Annonymous, Alison & Travis Spitzer, FB Foundation, Corrie Worth & Jim Kraxner, Charlynn & Robert Porter, Paul Rochford & Michael Violante, Nancy Baumer, Donna & Paul Yeoham, Robie & Fallon Vaughn, Bill Jones III, Steve & Maureen Kerrigan, Susan Corn-Wainright, Kathy & Bob Styer, Anne & John Ryan, Caryn Clayman, Gwen & Whit Hudson, Lisa Posin, Lisa Whiton Parker, Billy Sowers, David & Cindy Didawick, Andy & Cindy Russell, John & Carol Walter, Brenda & Lester Crain, Lance Sherman & Susan Buckley, Brent Leonard & Sean Webb, Fiona Druckenmiller, The Washowitz Family, Shelley & Michael Carr, Gigi Kemp, Donna Childs, Childers-King Family, Heather Evitts, Pho Phimvongsa, Rohit D'Souza & Alba Blanco, Deidra Smith, Dick & Nancy Wiederhorn, Joanie Eiland, Thomas & Ingred Edelman, Staci Christie, Lois Martin, Erin Pariser, Andy Main, Lise Gander Main, Lori Cappello, Craig Burr, Leslie Howa, Greg & Marilyn Brown, Diane & Chris Calkins, Scott Steiglitz, Diane Bettencourt, Nicole Fogel, Aaron Alan, Alan Bloom, Lexie Ellsworth, Betsy Collins, Thomas & Barbara Steinmetz, Rhonnie Leonard, Donna Gruneich, Jan Seligman, Peter & Heidi Hatch, Syliva Steding, Roger Thieme, Linda Spivak, Ed Snider, Missy Hargraves, Lynda Pearl, Sally Fuegi, Claire Beck, Candy & Walt Brett, Carol Linton, Karla Draper, Whitney Kroenke, Bill & Carrie Shoaf, Kathie & Scott Amann, Annette Steiner, Jamie-Lynn Sigler, Jennifer Steinwurtzel, Carole Lewis, Anna Haworth, Bleecker Springs, Anat Madanes, Eric & Ronnie Hoffman, Eric & Meagan Olson, Stephanie Perenchio, Cindy & Dave Barnard, Toni Bloomberg, Karen Brown, Susan Himes, Bob Pantermuehl, Melissa Shearn, Bernadette Leiweke, Michelle Rosen, Peggy Bergmann, Karen Roney, Michael Ostrow, Roger Stoker, George Griffith, Timothy Wagner, Sloan Barnett, Bettina Whyte, Pamela Graham, Solveig Magnusdottir, Bogi Palsson, Jan Oltman, Diane & Roger with Yogi, Karen Lord, Cary Collins, William & Kristy Woolfolk & Wendy Cohen

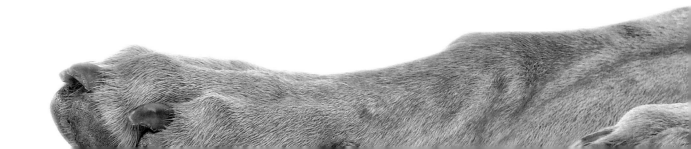

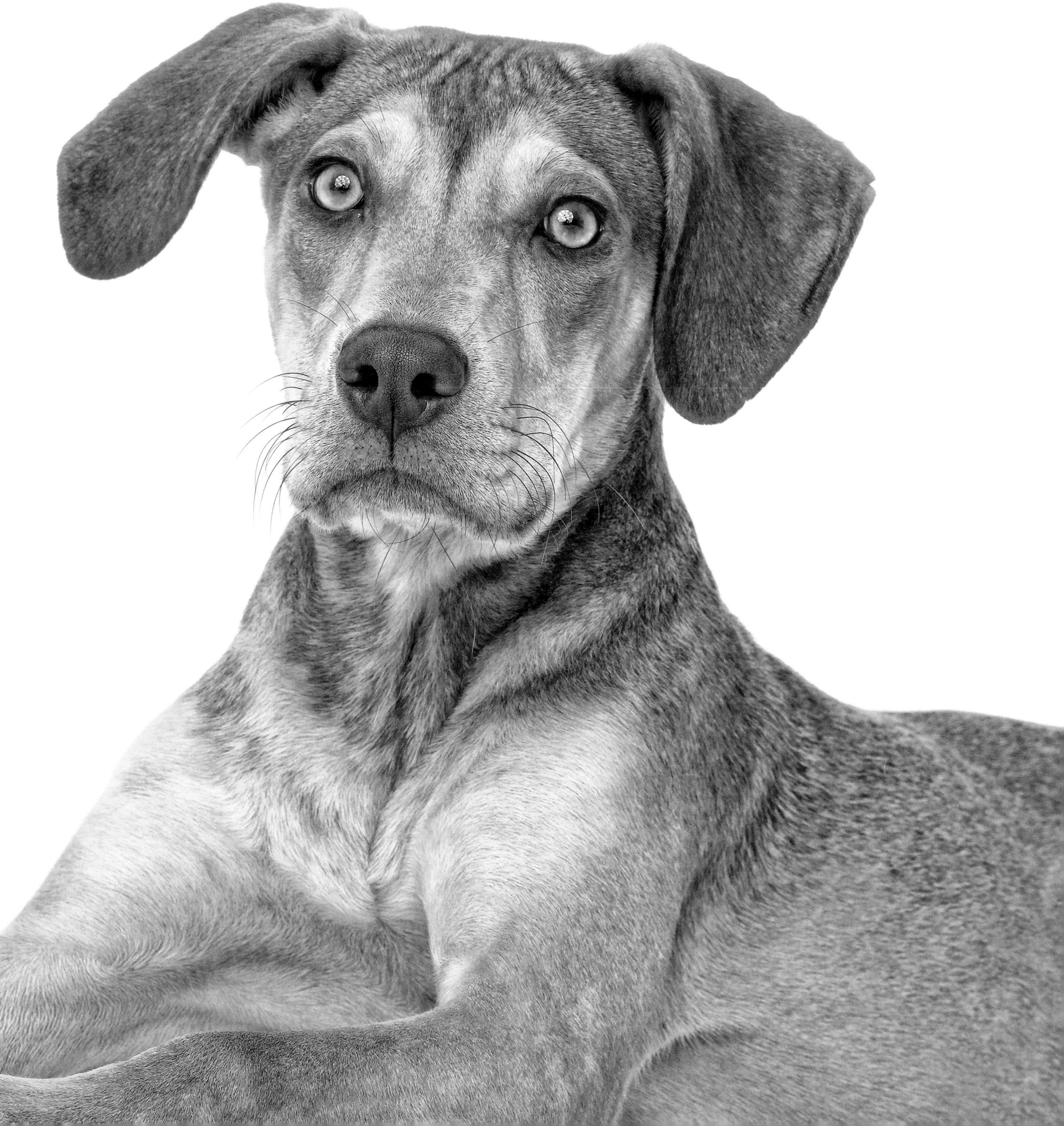

Homeless in 2013

About the images

The bloopers

Photographing dogs is not easy. While some dogs enjoy being photographed, it can take a few hours to get a camera-shy dog to surrender just two or three focused and compelling shots for Andrew.

It's not easy to photograph dogs in the studio. They move fast. They blink. They lick. They scratch. They pant. They sniff. They bark. They yawn. They worry. They drool. They become suspicious. They get excited.

Some don't like the unusual feel of the vinyl floor. Some don't like the sounds of the camera. Some don't like it when Andrew's face disappears behind his large camera. And some are afraid of the sound or flash of the huge studio lights. That's when things become difficult.

While most dogs don't notice the bright flash of the studio lights needed to illuminate them, Andrew has encountered a few dogs who jump virtually every time the scary strobes are fired. Not surprisingly, these dogs are also afraid of lightning and thunderstorms.

In some cases, the dog quickly makes the association between the flash and Andrew when he presses the button on his "lightning machine." When that happens, it's nearly impossible for Andrew to compose, focus and get the perfect shot, as the dog will run off each and every time Andrew holds up the camera.

One such dog was Maverick from Sun Valley, Idaho. Maverick bolted off the set each time Andrew held up his camera and fired the strobe. Maverick's owner simulated the process at home with the hope that some gentle training would help the yellow lab overcome his fear of the camera. Instead, Maverick now runs from the room whenever anyone holds up their hand and says "Click!"

How the amazing *Rover* images were made

Capturing the perfect expression to portray the unique personality of a dog in a single photograph takes some luck, an ability to compose quickly, creativity and a lot of patience. Capturing the stunning detail requires truly extraordinary equipment.

"I wanted to create images so lifelike, it would appear that the dogs could leap off the pages and into your lap. Mamiya Leaf professional digital photography solutions allow me to capture virtually every hair and whisker. Those tiny details add a texture to the image and bring the dogs to life inside Rover." - Andrew Grant

All images in *Rover* were captured on the Leaf Aptus 17 Aptus-II 7 high-resolution medium format digital backs on the Mamiya 645AFD II and DF camera systems for optimal color accuracy, stunning clarity and an unrivaled 12-stop dynamic range of tonal contrast.

The *Rover* dogs were lit with Profoto strobes and light-shaping tools that produce light that's crisp enough to create texture, gentle enough to create shape and big enough to capture all the life reflecting in their eyes.

Special thanks

Thank you
Rover could not have been produced without the tireless friendship, support, guidance, sense of humor, patience and talents of Amanda Hedlund.

Thanks to our families, friends, marketing partners, retailers, media and all of those who have made us feel at home while traveling across the country for two years. Special thanks to Ellen DeGeneres, Joey Ludwiczak, Heidi Klum, Ewan McGregor, Bruce Weber, Ted & Lynn Leonsis, Marti Huizenga, Jerry Penacoli, Jeremy Spiegel, Nancy Ryder, Barb Sherwood, Joanna Going, David Ciani, Kristine Hedlund, Kelly O'Donovan, Mark Miller, Team One, Hamid Nikkho, Mario Lopez, John & Kelly Ankwicz, Janice Feldman, Barbara Kildow, Donna Whitaker, Lisa McCarthy, Georgia Spogli, Christine Arme, Nathaniel Hedlund, Richelle Perez, Garrett Hedlund, Kirsten Dunst, Robert and Yvonne Hedlund, Cheryl Foerster, Gorsuch friends, Angie Callen, The Little Nell, Kelly Goodin, Kristine Hellman-Rosen, The Peaks Hotel, Harlan Bratcher, Toby Usnik, Kathy Tricomi, Cherie Wachter, Sarah Goodkin, Sara Davidson, Rachel Hahn, Anna Barbosa, Vivian Mayer, Tommy Post, Alisa Baur, David Roos, Claudia McMullin, Nick Winfrey, Joanne Horowitz, Hans & Kelly Brenninger, Virginia & Joe Schlegel, Jennifer Merry, Pamela Baynes, Zack Benson, Vladimir Medvinsky, Claudia Wattenberg, Cindy & Dave Barnard, Bonnie Atlas, Linda Vitale, Kathryn Fleck-Peisach, Heather Patterson, Jason Feinberg, Lauren Whitney, Jeff Zevely, Nadine Lipson, Maxine Russell, Samantha Bednar, David Ciani and of course, Greg Barbaccia.

Production credits

Concept & production by Andrew Grant
Photography by Andrew Grant
Fund raising by Amanda Hedlund
Marketing by Amanda Hedlund
Public relations by Amanda Hedlund
Dog wrangling by Amanda Hedlund
Photo editing by Andrew Grant
Graphic design by Andrew Grant
Rescue relations by Amanda Hedlund

Contact us

Andrew@AndrewGrantPhoto.com
Amanda@RoverToTheRescue.com

Shadow

Andrew's bio

Andrew Grant, known for his work in advertising, fashion, magazine and portrait photography, is now being nationally recognized for his special photography of dogs as subjects. Andrew's images of actors, authors, celebrities, kids, models, musicians and professional athletes ranging from Alicia Keys to Joe Montana have been featured in hundreds of advertisements, magazines, books and product packaging.

While Andrew continues his commercial photography, his attention now also includes capturing the beauty, grace and souls of all types of dogs—big, small, purebred and mixed, and most importantly, shelter rescues. His first book, *Rover* was featured on national television shows including *The Ellen DeGeneres Show* and *EXTRA*. Andrew began production of the second book, *Rover Woof Edition* when the first edition sold out in just a few months. Andrew raised over one million dollars for rescues while producing the books.

Andrew attended the renowned Brooks Institute of Photography in Santa Barbara, California. The Institute is regarded as one of the top three photography colleges in the world. Andrew is now based in San Diego, California.

Grant's philosophy is that great shots rarely just happen and that skilled photographers don't rely on luck to get the shot. He is a meticulous professional with years of experience, the technical skills and creativity needed to turn a creative director's conceptual vision into a compelling image.

"After I learned just how many dogs and cats enter shelters every year and the dramatic effect the recession and housing crisis was having on rescues, I began production of the first Rover book. There was an immediate sense of urgency, as I knew it would bring attention to the crisis."

"Pets provide us with unconditional love and priceless moments of joy. They ask only for a home in return. Let's work together and grant them that wish!"

– Andrew Grant

Commercial . Advertising . Fashion & Portrait Photography | AndrewGrantPhoto.com | A@AndrewGrantPhoto.com | 858.344.7900

ANDREWGRANTPHOTO.COM

Just some of the gear Andrew travels with to photograph the *Rover* dogs.

Andrew has photographed over 600 dogs in five years. He spends approximately 90 minutes with each pup in the studio.

ANDREWGRANTPHOTO.COM

It takes approximately one hour to prepare each image for print. Over 1,000 images have been published.

See **your** pet in *Rover*

Immortalize your best friend while helping homeless pets
Now you can have your dog photographed by Andrew and featured in a future edition of *Rover* when you make a donation to a benefiting rescue.

Be a hero to homeless pets
With your donation of $25,000, not only will your dog be a star in *Rover*, Andrew will also photograph and include four homeless pets. Now you and your dog can help other pets find their forever home.

We'll come to you
Andrew will capture your best friend's unique personality in a photo studio near your home.

See your dog on the cover
Want to make your dog famous? There's even a way to have your dog featured on the cover of the books you order or on the national cover.

Custom made greeting cards
Finely crafted note cards featuring your dog are available.

Prints for your home
Museum-quality prints from your dog's photo session are available for framing.

An extraordinary gift for the pet lover in your life
Looking for the perfect gift for the pet lover in your life? Put their best friend in *Rover*! Featuring their dog in a book is an extraordinary and unique gift they'll never forget and always cherish. Your loved one's dog will be photographed in a studio by Andrew and featured in a future edition of *Rover*.

All dogs are welcome
Most of the dogs featured in the *Rover* books once lived in a rescue or a shelter. However, we welcome all dogs (including purebreds).

For more information
Visit www.RoverToTheRescue.com

First published in the United States in 2014

Copyright © 2014 by Andrew Rauen

Library of Congress Control Number: 2009905951

ISBN 978-0-615-96155-2

Made in the USA

$95.00
ISBN 978-0-615-96155-2

59500>

9 780615 961552